HEART TO HEART WITH THE FATHER
A DEVOTIONAL SERIES

A SEEKING
HEART

BOOK 2

Clarice Fowler

To order additional copies of this book, contact:
Xlibris Corporation
1-888-795-4274
www.Xlibris.com
Orders@Xlibris.com
101131

Contents

My seeking heart . . .

*"'My soul thirsts for God, for the living God . . . My heart says of
You, 'Seek His face!' Your face, Lord will I seek . . . . I will study Your
commandments and reflect on Your ways . . . It is good to give thanks to
the Lord, to sing praises to the Most High . . . I am trusting You, O Lord,
saying, 'You are my God!'"*

*Psalm 42:2 (NIV), Psalm 27:8 (NIV), Psalm 119:15 (NLT), Psalm
92:1, 31:14 (NLT).*

My heavenly Father's heart . . .

*"'Are not two sparrows sold for a penny? Yet not one of them will fall to
the ground apart from the will of your Father . . . 'you are worth more
than many sparrows!' . . . The Lord is like a father to His children, tender
and compassionate to those who fear Him . . . The Lord is good to those
who depend on Him, to those who search for Him.'"*

Matthew 10;29, 31.(NIV). Psalm 103:13 (NLT). Lam. 3:25 (NLT) . . .

Dedication

To my son Chris and my daughter Jill.

Chris, you have been a great encouragement as I needed direction in writing this work. Your cover, for this book and the entire project, captures perfectly my heart and my love for God's creation. Thank you, for enthusiastically supporting me, when I needed your support and your strength when my strength was waning.

Jill, you have freely given of your time when I know you did not have it to give and painstakingly edited each and every day of my first book. You have continued reading through this manuscript as well. My heart is filled with joy as I realize how you uphold me as you watch me open up to learn more from our heavenly Father's heart.

To each of you, I can only give you a spirit full of gratitude and love from my heart to yours.

Acknowledgements

I want to express my deepest gratitude to the following special people without whom this work would not have gone forward.

Millie Barger, *who took on this project when I was very green as a writer. I will be forever grateful for all she has taught me.* **Nelda Davis,** *along with Millie are the only two who have edited all four books in this series. I am so very blessed to have these two ladies in my heart and life.*

Rosalyn Christopher, *my editor for "The Journey Begins" and "The Seeking Heart" projects, I offer my deepest gratitude. You have not only been my editor, but a true friend who has helped me not only on this work, but on many other ventures as well. Your joyful heart and support is such a blessing in my life. Words cannot express how much you mean to me.*

Kim Hefty, *my daughter-in-law, for permitting me to use the cover picture of the Swiss Alps, from your trip to Switzerland last year, on this project. You have made this an even richer experience for me as I will think of you every time I see this cover.*

Leeann Piering, *my editor for "A Seeking Heart" manuscript, how truly blessed I am for finding you and building a new friendship in my life. Your willingness to help me, not only with this book but also on computer issues, I can never repay, so I offer you my deepest gratitude and look forward to working with you in the future.*

Clarice Williams, *my namesake and friend, your meticulous job of checking the Scripture content of "The Seeking Heart" willingly and joyfully without complaint, made my job a joy and allowed me to move forward in my work. May God bless you richly for all you have done. What a joy you are in my life!*

Most of all, to my Lord and Savior Jesus Christ, *who is teaching me so much about seeking the heart of my Father in heaven. What a marvelous journey! To see Him work in such an amazing way through the releasing of the first book. He has taken it to places and people beyond anything that I could have envisioned. To God be all the glory! Now as I release this second book all praise, and honor goes to Him.*

Introduction

As I begin to reflect on the introduction to this, my second book, I cannot help but be reminded of how much my life has changed since I began writing this project in 2006.

My original manuscript was written in what I called our "home of peace" because our living room looked out on a sloped park-like setting that was very serene and reminded me of my Creator. This home was also, where the Lord uniquely bestowed upon me the content of this series. He continually poured out His blessing and the words flowed easily and extensively.

It began when my friend Diana gave me a devotional book for Christmas in 1999. My husband Don and I were living in a temporary situation where we were greatly needed to take care of his father. Don moved in with him in Salem, Oregon to help care for him and I kept the home-fires burning in our condominium in Newport, Oregon.

What we thought would be a temporary situation, turned into years. I will not go into all of the details about this period, (I already wrote about that in the introduction to book one), but God was doing a tremendous work in my life. He was shaping me into His will and purpose. Through the six years that Don and I were living this strange existence, God was directing us to move to this wonderful town near Salem, called Dallas.

As we were led to our wonderful home, we had to go through a stage where I lived in a unit of a triplex in Dallas, Oregon while my husband and his father moved to the unit next door. After being there for almost two years, we finally were all three able to move into this wonderful home under one roof. What a blessing!

I was very busy during that period caring for the three of us and was unaware of the work that God was preparing to do through me. It was not until after Dad passed on and I had some serious physical challenges that God was able to get my attention enough to guide me to write this book.

During the previous years, I underwent an arthroscopic procedure done on my right knee. After Dad went home to be with the Lord, my knee, which had been bothering me for some time, became worse. Physical therapy was no longer working so the doctor recommended another arthroscopic surgery. However, he did not promise a good outcome. Only our Lord knows why he did not recommend a knee replacement. Nevertheless, the surgery was unsuccessful so they fitted me with a complicated knee brace. At the time, I was wheel chair bound and could not walk without tremendous pain, so the brace allowed me some freedom. At least I could now drive and walk short distances but could not go shopping or walk for more than a few minutes, as the brace slipped and was cumbersome.

One day, I was listening to a sermon by Dr. Charles Stanley titled "How to get direction through fasting and prayer." I had a strong feeling that I needed to do that for the healing of my knee. Though I had never fasted and prayed for anything personal before, I called my daughter, who is in Christian ministry and had done that many times, to ask her advice. She immediately said "let's do it, Mom!" So that Tuesday I fasted and prayed for this healing and by 3:00 p.m. I was walking (no running) through the house and outside to show my husband the miracle that God had performed in my life. That was six years ago and I am still walking and enjoying life.

It was during this point in time that I revisited the devotional book that my friend had given me years before. I had not realized that I had written very meaningful notes. In the margin of each day, I had written the words "God is . . ." with a quality of God next to it. As I looked through that notebook, I was amazed to find that I had written 205 attributes about God the Father. This was incredibly amazing to me, as it had nothing to do with the devotional book I had read.

That was the beginning! I had a strong urge to continue to complete the remainder of those 365 days. It was not long before I felt God's nudge to start writing, using those titles. I did not know what God had in store for this work, but I knew it needed to be written. I had never written a book before so this was a stunning realization for me. It took several years before I understood that God had more for this work than just to share with my family. It is still remarkable to me that I am now working on the introduction to book two!

We no longer live in the home where God began this work. He has opened up a completely new chapter in our lives. God has guided my husband and me to live in a lovely retirement community in Dallas. We have been here a year as I write this, but I cannot begin to tell you what a blessing moving here is in our lives. The people, the staff, the facility are all beyond our expectations and my desire is to keep writing until the Lord has no more words for me to write.

As you read this book, you will notice that I have a sparrow on the cover of both books, (it will be on the next two books as well). When I was in my twenties, I lost two sisters in an automobile accident and I needed to be the strong one for my mother and my only other sister during that stressful time. God gave me the song, "His Eye Is on the Sparrow." It kept running steadily through my mind during that period and has been with me in all of my various life situations for fifty years. I wanted to offer praise back to God for giving me the wonderful gift of this song throughout my life.

I also wanted to make this book interactive because of the blessing it was for me to write my comments in a notebook—never realizing the impact it would become in my life. The "Your Reflections" at the bottom of each day provides you the opportunity to write your comments as well.

It is miraculous to me to look back and see how my heavenly Father directed this writing in such a profound way. I am astonished to be able to observe how beautifully the puzzle pieces of my life have come together. I glimpse how the hand of God has moved His work into one that is now in the homes of hundreds of people. I recently found out that it has been purchased in several countries around the world as well. I am very humbled by this and know that only God could take this book and multiply its readership. Only a living God could take an ordinary woman with a seeking heart and use her to further His kingdom work and I am very grateful for such a rich blessing!

Day 1

God is . . . Gentle

Bible Reading: Matthew 11:25-30

"Gentleness" is a quality that appears to have been lost, at least in our culture. Women strive to show everyone how strong and tough they can be, and almost regard the word "nice" as a negative quality.

When I was young, women were thought to be gentler than men were. Gentleness is a trait that I, as a woman, respect very much. Jesus described Himself as gentle. We read in verse 29, "Take my yoke upon you and learn from Me, for I am gentle and humble in heart, and you will find rest for your souls" (NIV).

Whenever I think of gentleness, I think of the animal world. One of the gentlest animals is a baby lamb. Maybe that is why Christ described Himself as gentle. He is, "The Lamb of God who takes away the sins of the world." He not only takes our sins upon Himself, but every burden, care and concern that we have. He will carry them all for us. He makes a brutal world, gentle. He who is master over everything, who stills the stormy waters, will make our stresses gentle if we only come to Him and ask Him.

He was the strongest of all humans, yet He was also gentle and humble. He feared no one yet told the little children to come to Him. He loves unconditionally, yet hates sin and unrighteousness. He told His followers that in order to be strong leaders they must also be humble servants to each other.

John 13:13-15 reads, "You call Me 'Teacher' and 'Lord' and rightly so, for that is what I am. Now that I, your Lord and Teacher, have washed your feet, you also should wash one another's feet. I have set you an example that you should do as I have done for you"' (NIV). What an example! If we are to show others the way of the cross, we must also become gentle and humble, to assure that we are showing them Christ and not how wonderful we are! Yes, gentleness is definitely a quality I desire!

Personal Note:

Gentleness and humility are two attributes as I write, that I want to keep in front of me at all times. I want to be sure that this is all of God's work and none of mine. I trust that as you go with me on my journey that you will see how God is working His work in me, to mold me into the image of Christ. I trust that you will see spiritual growth as day by day He helps me to reach toward Him and fall humbly at His feet in praise and adoration for all He is doing in my life.

I don't understand why my Father has called me to openly show you my struggles as well as my victories; I only know that to follow the Master wholly, I must become humble and gentle in spirit, then I truly will have rest for my soul.

Prayer:

Father, You are so gentle and loving to me. How I thank You and praise You for daily helping me to move ever closer to You. I thank You, my gentle Savior, for loving me so much that You paid the ultimate price for me. In Jesus' name I pray, Amen.

Your Reflections:

Day 2

God is . . . Our Dream Maker

Bible Reading: I Samuel 1:9-18

Hannah was a woman whom I have always admired. Her life was very hard. She was one of the two wives of Elkanah and she was barren. We have heard the same scenario repeatedly throughout the Old Testament.

Peninnah was the other wife and she had sons. She would taunt Hannah unmercifully, especially after Elkanah would go to the temple for his yearly sacrifice and bring back the rest of the meat to share with his family.

Each time he would give Hannah the choicest piece of meat. Peninnah would mock and ridicule Hannah until she would leave in tears, not even eating her share. Elkanah would go in and try to comfort Hannah, but she was so broken-hearted over not having any children that she could not be comforted.

Hannah did not give up on God, however. One particularly hard time she got up, left, and went to the temple to pray. She was so distraught that Eli, the priest, thought that she was drunk. He went to her and told her to throw away the wine. She humbly told him that she was not drunk but was praying out of anguish and sorrow. Samuel wrote; "In that case, Eli said, go in peace! May the God of Israel grant the request you have asked Him" I Samuel 1:17 (NLT).

God knew Hannah's dream! She just had to be patient and wait for His timing. She eventually became the mother of Samuel. She told God that if He gave her a child she would dedicate him to His service. God mercifully gave her a son. "Meanwhile the boy Samuel grew taller and grew in favor with the Lord and with the people" I Samuel 2:26 (NLT). She kept her promise to God and gave up her son who was raised in the temple and set aside for a special work that God had preordained. It had been about three centuries since God had spoken directly to man. Nevertheless, Samuel found favor with Him and God was able again to have a man to whom He could speak audibly. Samuel was used mightily by God and was the last of the judges.

Personal Note:

I love this story because Hannah was the first woman that I know of, that God told to give up her son. That was her dream! Did God, however, forget her dream? No! He never does! He always out-gives us. Hannah did the hardest thing a mother could do. She gave up her only son so that he might serve God.

However, God gave her three more sons and two daughters. What a blessing! What a dream come true! God will fulfill our dreams as well! Nevertheless, it will be in His timing and in His plan! He alone knows when to make our most precious dreams come true. He will reward any one who commits their lives into His care, and He will do it far beyond what we could ask or think. He is our overflowing dream maker!

Prayer:

Father, how fabulous You are! Please help me to be patient and wait for Your fulfillment. I know that when I trust You, You not only give me the desires of my heart, but You surpass anything that I could ever dream. I praise You for Your abundant promises and provisions. In Jesus' name, Amen.

Your Reflections:

Day 3

God is . . . Persevering

Bible Reading: Luke 18:1-8

My husband can fix almost anything. He is very resourceful and often duct tape is his remedy. If this tape will work, he will not hesitate to use it. In fact, for his seventieth birthday, we surprised him with a duct tape party. Our son made a cake that looked like a roll of duct tape. Everyone brought him duct tape for a present. I think that may have been his favorite birthday!

The reason he can be so resourceful is that he knows how to persevere. He will seldom give up until he has the solution to whatever it is that needs to be fixed. How I respect this quality in him! I think this is one reason there are so many examples throughout Scripture pertaining to patience, persistence and perseverance.

Jesus used a wonderful example in Luke 18. He told His disciples a story to show that they should always pray and never give up. He told them about a widow who went to a judge who was not very caring about either God or people. She begged him to bring justice to her in a dispute she was having. He ignored her for a while, but she kept persisting until she finally wore him down, and he judged her case just to get rid of her.

Too often, we give up praying for something, perhaps right before God is ready to answer it. He wants us to keep on, keeping on! Perseverance is one way that we are assured that we are truly turning our problems over to our Father and leaving it in His hands.

Otherwise, it is too easy to take it back and try to solve it ourselves. Diligence brings great humility, a quality that our Father loves!

God is amazingly persevering with us. It is not that God does not hear us immediately, but when we continue to bring a problem to Him, He likes to persist until the end. Paul wrote, "Patient endurance is what you need now, so that you will continue to do God's will. Then you will receive all that He has promised" Hebrews 10:36 (NLT). What a wonderful objective! I am continually pressing toward that goal in my prayer life.

Personal Note:

When I started on this journey six years ago, I could hardly persevere on anything in my prayer time except the very basic things like consistently praying for someone's salvation God has tested me to the limits in these six years.

When it comes to asking for His help and waiting for His reply, I am much more patient and persistent than I used to be. He has shown me repeatedly how trustworthy He is. Therefore, I can depend on His answer. I do not like to wait as long as it takes sometimes, but I am grateful to Him that I can feel secure in knowing that He will answer, no matter what the situation. I am learning, ever so slowly, to keep asking until I receive an answer or clear direction from Him. I know beyond any doubt that He has heard my cry and help is on the way!

Prayer:

Thank You, Father for always hearing and answering my prayers. When I am anguishing over something, Father, Your heart anguishes along with me. You alone know my future and what is best in my life. Help me to keep persevering as I wait and grow in You. In the name of Jesus, Amen.

Your Reflections:

Day 4

God is . . . My Anguish-Bearer

Bible Reading: Matthew 26:36-45

Have you ever-felt anguish of soul? Jesus did. No one has yet felt a deeper sorrow, hurt, pain, or anguish than our Lord. You and I go through some deep waters at times. Our spirit can be crushed and broken and we feel like we cannot bear the brokenness any longer. Our body, mind and spirit feel like we cannot take any more hurt. When we are this broken, we have confidence in knowing that our Savior bore all of our sorrow, pain and anguish so that we would not have to carry it alone.

When He was in the Garden of Gethsemane, He told His disciples that they were to stay where they were, and pray. "My soul is crushed with grief to the point of death. Stay here and keep watch with me. He went on a little farther and bowed with His face to the ground, praying, My Father! If it is possible, let this cup of suffering be taken away from Me. Yet, I want Your will to be done, not mine!" Matthew 26:38-39 (NLT).

What a prayer! In His humanness, He did not want to suffer what He knew He must live through. Nevertheless, His godly spirit and soul wanted His Father's perfect will to be done. He was so selfless, that even though He knew that He was carrying every agony and care that we have ever experienced, He was willing to go through it all, for us. There is a song that I love which is titled, "He Could Have Simply Walked Away"—what if He had?

Have you ever thought about where we would be today if Jesus had not loved us so much that He was willing to bear the deepest misery a human can endure? However, His will was to please the Father. "For God's will was for us to be made holy by the sacrifice of the body of Jesus Christ, once for all time" Hebrews 10:10 (NLT). Therefore, Jesus went through it all, every sin that our evil humanity could ever think of, and He did it for us! What a Savior!

Personal Note:

I have thought about what life would be like, if Jesus had not been our anguish-bearer. Would I even exist today? History has proven how corrupt our selfish nature is without any morality or purpose. We probably would have blown each other up long ago if left to our own devices.

However, God, in His mercy, had the perfect plan and knew His Son's heart. He knew that His Son was well aware of how important His mission was. Nevertheless, Jesus was still given a human choice. His love was so deep—that even knowing what He must face, He never turned back—He went through it all. Even if it had been just for me, He would have done it! I cannot even imagine that kind of love, but I am so very, very grateful!

Prayer:

Father, what love You bestow upon me that You sent Your Son to the cross to pay my penalty for sin. How I love You, Jesus! I cannot thank You enough for going through it all for me. Thank You for not "simply walking away." I praise You, in Your precious name, the name of Jesus! Amen.

Your Reflections:

Day 5

God is . . . The Written Word

Bible Reading: 2 Peter 1:16-21

Throughout the ages, one of the most powerful tools that God has given us concerning Himself is the written Word. In the Old Testament He spoke through godly men and the prophets, and in the New Testament He spoke through godly men and the apostles. Peter tells us, "Above all, you must realize that no prophecy in Scripture ever came from the prophet's own understanding, or from human initiative. No, those prophets were moved by the Holy Spirit, and they spoke from God" 2 Peter 1:20-21 (NLT).

Peter makes it clear that what He says is true. He reminds us that he, Peter, saw the Lord transformed in His heavenly body. "We saw His majestic splendor with our own eyes when He received honor and glory from God the Father. The voice from the majestic glory of God said to Him, 'This is My dearly loved Son, who brings Me great joy" 2 Peter 1: 16b-17 (NLT).

That event was when Jesus took Peter, James and John up on a mountain. There they saw the glory of God come down, and Jesus was transfigured before their eyes. They saw two men come down and the three disciples recognized them as Moses and Elijah. Peter, who always spoke first and thought later, wanted to build three monuments to capture the event. When God spoke, the disciples were terrified and fell face down on the ground. As soon as this event happened, a cloud covered Moses and Elijah, and when the disciples recovered, only Jesus was standing there. I am not sure that they really understood what had happened until after the resurrection of Jesus.

Peter wanted to remind the early church of the authenticity of this miraculous event, which he witnessed. He wanted to be sure that there was a record. Apparently, Jesus had allowed Peter to know that his earthly life was almost over, so Peter wanted to be certain that there was a written accounting of proof that Jesus was who He said He was. Without the writings of history, we would have little knowledge of past events.

How blessed we are that God was so thorough in His accounting of all of the events since the beginning of time. It is not only important to us, but it is part of who God is and His story! In Deuteronomy 6:6, 9 (NLT) we read, "You must commit yourselves wholeheartedly to these commands that I am giving you today. Write them on the doorposts of your house and on your gates." Yes, God's written word is that important!

Personal Note:

As I am growing in the Lord, I am coming to realize that the best gift I can pass on to my children is the written word. I guess that is one reason God gave me this format with my personal notes. Even though at times, it brings to light my vulnerabilities, I also realize that it gives my children insight into my heart.

The other truth is that I have not memorized as much of God's Word as I would like to. Therefore, I am starting afresh and making it a priority to write His Word on the doorposts of my heart, so that I will not forget anything that He has for me.

Prayer:

Father, thank You for Your faithfulness in providing me with Your Word, so that I may remember everything that You have done

for me! Help me to read, study, and memorize Your Word that I may grow closer to You and to Your heart. In my Savior's name, Amen.

Your Reflections:

Day 6

God is . . . The Divine Revelation

Bible Reading: Hebrews 1:1-5

The Bible is very interesting because there are many ways it assures me that it is truly God's Word. Some of these are the revelations that were written, thousands of years before they came true. Daniel saw things that he had no way to describe in his day. As he saw his visions, he must have wondered what all of this really meant. He was so amazed by what he saw, that at the end of his revelation from God he was overcome, and laid sick for several days. He saw things that we, with all our technology, have not yet experienced.

Aside from the written Word, the greatest revelation that God ever sent was His precious Son, Jesus the Christ. He is the Divine Revelation. When Jesus was here on earth, He tried to reveal everything that He could, but the vast majority of us simply did not understand. He had a precise work to do. He was to become the ultimate sacrifice for our sin, so that He could complete God's purpose. Since Jesus revealed Himself to us, we who believe can now have free access to the Father through the Son. The communication line is open again between God and humanity. We are heirs and joint heirs with Christ.

We read in Hebrews, "Long ago, God spoke many times and in many ways to our ancestors through the prophets. Now in these final days, He has spoken to us through His Son. God promised everything to the Son as an inheritance, and through the Son He created the universe" Hebrews 1:1-2 (NLT). Paul gives us another wonderful promise in Hebrews, "For if we are faithful to the end, trusting God just as firmly as when we first believed, we will share in all that belongs to Christ" Hebrews 3:14 (NLT). What an awesome promise!

Personal Note:

I am very thankful that God was thorough in giving us divine direction and revelations throughout the Bible. The more I read and study God's Word, the more clarity and blessing I receive. God wants me to have a very understandable picture of His plan and purpose for me. God's plan is that I accept Jesus Christ as my Lord and Savior. His purpose is that I praise and glorify Him and live my life in such a way that I draw others to want to know more about the mighty God I serve. He loves us so generously that He wants every human being to accept His plan of salvation and live with Him eternally. I am enormously grateful that I accepted "The Divine Revelation," Jesus Christ as my personal Savior! How merciful He is!

Prayer:

Father, thank You for sending the "Divine Revelation," Your blessed Son, to die as a sacrifice for my sin. I praise You with a thankful heart that You now include me in Your family because I have received Jesus Christ as my atonement for every sin that I have ever committed. In His marvelous name, Amen.

Your Reflections:

Day 7

God is . . . My Example of Perfect Timing

Bible Reading: Luke 1:18-25

God's timing is amazing! However, we are not always in agreement with His "right time." This was the case with Zechariah. He was a priest at the time of Herod the King. His wife's name was Elizabeth. God found them righteous in His eyes, but they had no children and had always wanted them.

Zechariah was serving his term in the temple and as he was praying, Gabriel, the Arch Angel, appeared and told him that he was going to have a child in his old age. Zechariah had his doubts so the angel struck him mute until after the baby was born.

Zechariah and Elizabeth had tried their whole lives to have a child, but it was not God's perfect timing until they were both too old to have children. They were in the same position as Abraham and Sarah and no doubt had studied about them countless times, but when it came time for God to bring them a child in their old age, Zechariah doubted. How crucial this perfectly timed event was in the archives of history. Their son was John the Baptist who was the forerunner of Christ.

It is easy for us to doubt God's timing in our lives, as well. We pray for something dear to our hearts and we expect God to answer immediately. Years may go by with what seems like no answer, however God's timing is often very different from the limited life span, which we use to judge time.

Little did Zechariah and Elizabeth ever dream that God would use them to provide the messenger who would prepare the way for the coming of the long awaited Messiah! Paul wrote, "When we were utterly helpless. Christ came at just the right time and died for us sinners" Romans 5:6 (NLT). Yes, God's timing is perfect, every time!

Personal Note:

From my journal on October 1, 2000: "It is encouraging to read in history how each piece of God's amazing puzzle has been fulfilled. God gave specific times and directions to the prophets. Whether it was good or bad news, God fulfilled the prophecy in His timing and He always will."

God forever has a time line. When we look back, we can see how everything fits so beautifully. Nevertheless, when we are going through deep waters or hard places, it is very difficult to see His hand at work and trust Him to bring about His will in His precise timing.

I have found great personal encouragement in writing this blessing today. It is easy to doubt, like Zechariah but in that same chapter, Luke wrote, "Elizabeth gave a glad cry and exclaimed to Mary, God has blessed you above all women and your child is blessed . . . You are blessed because you believed that the Lord would do what He said" Luke 1:42, 45 (NLT). Mary never doubted. She had complete trust in her God!

Prayer:

Oh Father, what a wonderful role model You gave us, in choosing Mary to bring Your only begotten Son into the world. May I learn to trust Your timing, and have total faith in You. In the name of Your blessed Son, Jesus! Amen.

Your Reflections:

Day 8

God is . . . Reputable

Bible Reading: Ezekiel 12:21-28

I love proverbs, and two were often quoted by my mother and grandmother. "A stitch in time saves nine" was a favorite of my grandmother. My mother, on the other hand used "A watched pot never boils." There are many others, but these came immediately to my mind.

Israel had a proverb that was not a good one. It defamed the name of the Lord and He wanted it to stop. It was, "The days go by, and every vision comes to nothing" Ezekiel 12:22b (NIV). What a negative thing to be passed around concerning God's visions. God spoke to Ezekiel who wrote, "'This is what the Sovereign Lord says, 'I am going to put an end to this proverb, and they will no longer quote it in Israel'" Ezekiel 12:23 (NIV).

This prophecy would happen immediately. "The word of the Lord came to me: 'Son of man, if a country sins against me by being unfaithful and I stretch out my hand against it to cut off its food supply and send famine upon it and kill its men and animals, even if these three men . . . Noah, Daniel and Job were in it, they could save only themselves by their righteousness, declares the Sovereign Lord'" Ezekiel 14:12-14 (NIV).

We need to be very careful as His followers that we do not damage the name of our Lord, either in action or in word. God cares about how nations treat Him. Our nation was founded on Christian principles. We should do all we can, to see that those principles are continued in our country, before God withholds His hand of mercy from us.

The Psalmist wrote, "Now then, you kings act wisely. Be warned you rulers of the earth! Serve the Lord with reverent fear, and rejoice with trembling. Submit to God's royal Son, or He will be angry, and you will be destroyed in the midst of all your activities—for His anger flares up in an instant, but what joy for all who take refuge in Him!" Psalm 2:10-12 (NLT). How careful I want to be to hold this reputable God in highest esteem and respect. He will always keep His promise—I can count on that!

Personal Note:

Just like the Israelites of old, we have promises that are still to be fulfilled. I think every generation since Jesus was here on earth thought that His return would happen in their generation.

A big hype went around in the early 70's when we thought that His coming was eminent. Today, in part because of this, we have become complacent and apathetic. Many have just ignored the fact that Jesus will come again and they no longer think about the possibility that it could be in our generation.

If we are wise, we will be looking up and expecting Christ to come at any time. This is what He told us to do. I personally, am looking for Him to come at any moment, at His perfect timing, however, only the Father knows exactly when that will be. I hope it is soon!

Prayer:

Father, I pray that You will keep me in tune to Your promises. May I not become apathetic about the prophecies that have not yet come to completion. You are absolutely reputable in Your Word, and I trust You and Your truth. Thank You for never failing to fulfill any of Your promises. In my Savior's name, Amen.

Your Reflections:

Day 9

God is . . . The Pure Living Water

Bible Reading: John 4:10-15

God's creation is so full of beautiful water. Most of us love being around it. We enjoy the ocean with its might and power as we watch the waves come crashing to the seashore. We delight in a river, as it releases its flow in the mountains picking up speed as it goes through the valleys to empty its precious load in the sea. We are refreshed by a soft mountain brook, as it joyfully babbles its way over the rocks to empty into a quiet mountain lake. No matter what it is, we are drawn to it. It brings us peace and serenity.

God loves water! In fact, that is the first thing that He created. "In the beginning God created the heavens and the earth. The earth was formless and empty, and darkness covered the deep waters" Genesis 1:1-2 (NLT). When He had finished creating everything, He made Adam and Eve and placed them in the Garden of Eden. A river flowed in the middle of it and watered all of it. Everything God made was perfect and back then, the water was pure spring water.

Jesus, when He described Himself to the Samaritan woman at Jacob's well, said to her, "Anyone who drinks this water will soon become thirsty again. But those who drink the water I give will never be thirsty again. It becomes a fresh, bubbling spring within them, giving them eternal life" John 4:13-14 (NLT).

Water has always been used for cleansing. In John 4:10, Jesus said, "If you only knew the gift God has for you and who you are speaking to, you would ask me, and I would give you living water." (NIV). Jesus' blood is our cleansing stream bringing us that living water that flows through Him to us and washes away our sin. He is a fresh, bubbling spring within us and that is the purest and cleanest water of all!

Personal Note:

When I was a little girl, I always loved going anywhere there was water. Whether it was the mountains or the ocean as long as it had water, I was happy. I remember one year, I was probably five or six years old, my family decided that they would like to go to the massive redwoods in northern California. The beauty and the serenity of camping among those giant trees was so awesome to everyone except me. My mother asked me why I was not enjoying this exceptional beauty. I replied, "Mama, there is no water!" To me, nothing could be entirely beautiful unless it had water to experience.

I am still like that today. In this home, where we have beautiful fir and oak trees that give us the feeling of being in the mountains, my husband created a seven-tiered waterfall that comes crashing around a beautiful fir tree stump. I hear in the water the joyful sounds as it sends up its praises to the Creator of the Universe, who gave it such massive power and beauty.

We no longer live in that beautiful home with the magnificent waterfall, yet God has given me even more. We live in Dallas Retirement Village now, and feel so very blessed. We do not look out over water, instead we have a lovely park outside our window and God has brought me something more precious than the most beautiful water my mind could ever imagine. It is the Living water that bubbles up from my heart to my Father who gave me His Son, the Living Water!

Prayer:

Father, You are so precious to me! How I praise You for the beauty of the creation all around me. But most of all, I thank You for Jesus Christ, the living water, who cleansed me and made me spotless so that I could have eternal life. In His name, Amen.

Your Reflections:

Day 10

God is . . . Thinking Precious Thoughts

Bible Reading: Psalm 139:1-6

It is a fabulous thing to realize that God thinks about us all of the time. There is no masquerade with God. We may be able to put on a "good front" with our friends and families but God knows everything about us. This Psalm is such a blessing to me! "O Lord, You have examined my heart and know everything about me. You know when I sit down or stand up. You see me when I travel! And when I rest at home. You know everything about me. You know what I am going to say even before I say it, Lord" Psalm 139:1-4 (NLT).

He created us, He knows everything we can do, say or think! He knows our strengths and our weaknesses—good things and bad! Yet even if we feel we have failed Him, He loves us anyway! We never can hide from Him. There is not one thing that we could ever do that would keep Him from loving us!

People may have hurt us, or fallen short of our expectations and let us down, but God never will. He is patient with loving kindness. He is merciful, and caring! His thoughts are always on each of us, individually. I love the way verses 17-18 reads, "How precious are Your thoughts about me, O God. They cannot be numbered. I can't even count them, they outnumber the grains of sand! And when I wake up, You are still with me!" (NLT). It is hard to imagine the God of the universe thinking about each one of us so often that His thoughts outnumber the grains of sand! Amazing! What a marvelous God!

Personal Note:

If you have never read this incredible Psalm, I encourage you to do so. If you are struggling with low self-esteem, it will lift your spirit.

When I was a little girl, I was always taught never to think too highly of myself. That was almost the worst sin I could commit. My mother, I believe, had a healthy confidence. I am sure it was because of her love for the Lord. However, she was so afraid that I would become conceited that she squelched my creativity. I was not allowed to take "pride" in any of my accomplishments, at least verbally.

The good thing was however, I always knew there was a God who loved me. I just had trouble accepting how far-reaching His love extended. I did not have a good earthly father image to teach me what a loving father is like. No doubt, this led to my quest to know my heavenly Father more intimately.

I think many of us have similar misconceptions of our amazing heavenly Father. God makes it clear that we are all precious in His sight! He made us and formed us each unique, yet each just as precious. He delights in us! We are the apple of His eye!

Prayer:

How thankful I am to You, my Father, because You know my every thought and even more awesome You think of me so often. How grateful I am, to have such amazing love bestowed on me. I will praise Your name forever with deep gratitude and love for You. In Jesus' precious name, Amen.

Your Reflections:

Day 11

God is . . . A Giver of Double Portions

Bible Reading: 2 Kings 2:9-14

From the time I was a little girl, whenever I think of a double portion, I remember the Doublemint gum commercials. They were designed to make us think about a double portion of flavor.

God loves to grant double portions as well. Elijah had been an amazing instrument of God and Elisha wanted to be like him. As the two of them were walking along, Elijah asked Elisha what he could do for him before he was taken away into heaven.

In 2 Kings 2:9-11, the following is recorded: '"When they came to the other side, Elijah said to Elisha, 'tell me what I can do for you before I am taken away.' Elisha replied, 'please let me inherit a double share of your spirit and become your successor.' 'You have asked a difficult thing,' Elijah replied. 'If you see me when I am taken from you, then you will get your request. But if not, then you won't.' As they were walking along and talking, suddenly a chariot of fire appeared, drawn by horses of fire. It drove between the two men, separating them, and Elijah was carried by a whirlwind into heaven. Elisha saw it and cried out, 'My Father! My Father! I see the chariots and charioteers of Israel. And as they disappeared from sight, Elisha tore his clothes in distress"' (NLT).

Of all of the things that Elisha could have asked, his eyes were already on the things of God. He wanted to double the effectiveness of Elijah—to have double of Elijah's spirit toward God!

God will always honor us, anytime that we want more of Him. The very first miracle happened immediately after Elijah was taken up into heaven.

In 2 Kings 2:13-14 we read, "Elisha picked up Elijah's cloak, which had fallen when he was taken up. Then Elisha returned to the bank of the Jordan River. He struck the water with Elijah's cloak and cried out, 'where is the Lord the God of Elijah?' Then the river divided and Elisha went across'" (NLT). Elisha dared to ask the impossible and God was quick to answer him! God loves to mete out double of what we ask when we seek Him according to His purpose for us.

Personal Note:

I have gone through most of my life without realizing that God is just waiting for me to ask Him for a double portion of His spirit within me. As I am writing these notes, I am asking God to double His portion in this work, blessing it, to touch lives in all different circumstances and at different places in their walk with Him. I finally understand that He will use this in a very powerful way.

I am picking up the cloak of all of the competent writers before me, and asking God to use this ordinary woman's work knowing that He is moving my fingers in the directions that He wants written. He must want it in print in the style that only I can write. Why, is beyond my comprehension. I am just the vehicle that He is using in this way, and He needs my personality, my style and my fingers to complete His purpose in this work. Praise to His holy name!

Prayer:

Oh Father, all You ever want from any of us is to say, "use me." You are so generous in all Your dealings with us. I am asking You

in Your precious name to use *me* in whatever way You want. Thank You for Your mighty works and a double portion of Your blessing! In Jesus' name, Amen.

Your Reflections:

Day 12

God is . . . Our Destiny Maker

Bible Reading: I Kings 1:1-4, 2:13-24

Have you ever wondered why you were born at this particular time in history? Why you live in this country instead of another? I am grateful to my Father for caring so much about me that He chose me to be born in this time and place and the perfect generation for me.

Each of us is born at the very best age in time to fulfill God's destiny for us. We read in the Psalms, "You saw me before I was born. Everyday of my life was recorded in Your book. Every moment was laid out before a single day had passed" Psalm 139:16 (NLT). Nothing about my life is a mistake. Every detail God had recorded in His book.

A young girl was born in the time when David was king. She may have wondered at times, why she was born at this crucial time. Her name was Abishag. King David was getting very old and he was so cold that no matter how many blankets they put on him, he could not keep warm. His advisors suggested that he find a young virgin to look after him and lie beside him to keep him warm, so they searched the kingdom for just the right girl. Abishag was chosen. "The girl was very beautiful and she looked after the king and took care of him. But the king had no sexual relations with her" I Kings 1:4 (NLT).

She was only his companion for a few months before he died. After his death, there was an attempt from Solomon's brother,

Adonijah, to try to take the kingdom away from Solomon. One of the underhanded things that he wanted was for Solomon to grant that he marry Abishag. Adonijah was not doing this out of love but as a sly move to take over the kingdom. Having Abishag as his wife would put him in a good position to overthrow his brother Solomon and become king.

Abishag might just as well have been an old discarded piece of furniture, even though she was still young and a virgin. She was now a part of King David's harem, so she would belong to the future King. Solomon saw right through his brother's plan and had Adonijah killed for disloyalty to him. I am sure that Abishag had no idea that her life would be recorded in the most famous book of all times, the Holy Bible. However, even though her role was not significant as we judge it, it was important enough so that God wanted this event recorded.

We never know what or how God will use us in life. We may feel that we do not make a difference but to God, we all have a purpose, "For I know the plans I have for you, declares the Lord, plans to prosper you and not to harm you, plans to give you hope and a future" Jeremiah 29:11 (NIV). I cannot help but think that Abishag lived a pampered life in the harem of King Solomon. I believe that he remembered how well she took care of his father. I do not think Adonijah would have been so kind!

Personal Note:

Sometimes we can feel like we are just a doormat for people to walk all over, or just an object to be used, or we just wander aimlessly and wonder why we are here, but God has a plan and a purpose for each of us, in this time frame and in this place. We just need to trust Him with our whole heart and let Him show us what He has for us.

I cannot even imagine what God still has in store for me. He keeps taking me to a higher and higher plane as I climb upward, one-step at a time. Each day I become more amazed as I keep walking up the mountain. Each vista is so incredible that I cannot imagine what the next one will be like. I only know that I am to keep walking and following His plan. My destiny is in His hands!

Prayer:

O Father, You hold me carefully and gently in Your hands. I thank You that I don't know the future because I'm sure that if I did, I might quit walking and cower behind a shrub in fear. But I know that You have my destiny all planned out for me. How grateful I am, my blessed Lord! Keep me just walking a step at a time. In Your wonderful Name, the name of Jesus! Amen.

Your Reflections:

Day 13

God is . . . The Final Word

Bible Reading: Habakkuk 2:12-17

Why does the Lord allow terrorism in our world? It has happened throughout history and we seldom learn from history. Habakkuk was a man of questions, living in a violent time in history where it seemed that the evil was winning. He was not afraid to confront God head on! In chapter one we find him asking God direct questions like, "Must I forever see these evil deeds? Why must I watch all this misery? Wherever I look, I see destruction and violence. I am surrounded by people who love to argue and fight. The law has become paralyzed, and there is no justice in the courts" Habakkuk 1:3-4 (NLT).

God then answers Habakkuk. "Write My answers plainly on tablets, so that a runner can carry the correct message to others. This vision is for a future time. It describes the end, and it will be fulfilled. If it seems slow in coming, wait patiently, for it will surely take place. It will not be delayed" Habakkuk 2:2b-3 (NLT).

I think I keep referring to the book of Habakkuk because it is so relevant to our times. We are living daily in these kinds of situations, as we get closer to our Lord's coming. Even as Christians, we have become somewhat apathetic about the Lord coming back to earth. I think this small book can bring us to our knees and beg the Lord's mercy as we approach the end of this age. Verse 14 brings us hope in these treacherous times. "For as the waters fill the sea, the earth will be filled with an awareness of the glory of the Lord!" (NLT). No matter how bad it gets, our God is in control! He is the final Word. All praise to Him who holds the world in His sovereign hands!

Personal Note:

The stage is set for more and more violence to take place, as we approach the end times. There is not a nation in the world that is not affected by it. Israel sits in the center of all of the terrorist groups, whose mission is to destroy her as a nation. Nevertheless, God has promised that even though times get extremely bad, He will always provide a remnant out of Israel. That was His covenant with Abraham, Isaac and Jacob, and it is the same today.

I feel my personal obligation to pray for the peace of Jerusalem as the Bible directs, as well as the nation of Israel. This tiny nation is the hub of spiritual warfare, but it is also the apple of God's eye. I will commit myself anew to pray for them as well as all of the democracies around the world that God's mercy will be upon us all. He is in control of everything that happens in the world. He is the final Word!

Prayer:

Father, You have spoken to my heart about being more faithful to pray for Your chosen people as they are bombarded on every side by evil. Help me to be consistent in doing so, until Jesus comes to end the conflict. In His name I pray, Amen.

Your Reflections:

Day 14

God is . . . My Provision

Bible Reading: Ruth 2:1-8

So many things seem to "just happen" in our lives. We have two schools of thought. We can either think, what a coincidence, or we can thank God and say, what a blessing. Most of the time, many of us think that these life happenings are just a coincidence. But are they? If we believe that God has an ultimate purpose and plan for us, would it not also seem probable that He should allow all things to work together for our good?

Ruth was an excellent example of this. She was from the country of Moab that was an enemy, or at least at odds, with Israel. She had come all the way to a foreign land to be with her mother-in-law, who apparently was a huge influence in her life. They were both widows and were among the poor. Ruth wanted to help wherever she could, so she just remarked to her mother-in-law that she would like to go out to the fields after the harvesters were done, and pick up the remnants of grain that the harvesters left behind for the poor to pick up. This was a normal practice among the rich. Some being more generous than others.

"So Ruth went out to gather grain behind the harvesters. And it happened that she found herself working in a field that belonged to Boaz, the relative of her father-in-law, Elimelech". Ruth 2:3 (NLT). What a coincidence, or was it? She did not know that this field belonged to a strategic relative of her mother-in-law. He was in the position to be a kinsman redeemer. Whenever someone died in Israel, it was the law that the closest relative could redeem the widow and marry her. Boaz was second in line to marry Ruth if he so chose.

Through a series of divine interventions, God brought every detail together and Boaz and Ruth were married. It was through the line of Boaz that we had King David and through David, our Lord and Savior Jesus Christ. "So Boaz took Ruth and she became his wife. Then he went to her and the Lord enabled her to conceive and she gave birth to a son. They named him Obed. He became the father of Jesse, and the grandfather of King David" Ruth 4:13, 17 (NLT). Coincidence? I don't think so!

Personal Note:

Does God have a purpose in all of our lives? I believe that He does. I believe that every day of my life, God is making things happen for my good. I have seen Him work too many things out that should not have worked, to think otherwise.

Do you ever pray and thank the Lord for the blessing of that parking place right close to the store when it is pouring down rain? I do! One specific time I was working as a knitting instructor for a craft store and it was located in a strip mall. Parking was always a challenge. This particular day, I was not feeling up to par, it was raining hard and I had many things that I had to carry into the store to teach my class.

Before I arrived, I prayed simply that the Lord would open up a parking space close enough that I would be able to carry everything in without getting soaked, and all my knitting supplies soaked as well. As I came to the store, sure enough, there was a person just pulling out right in front of the store. I said a quick thank You to my Father and proceeded to park.

That would have been a phenomenal answer as it was, however when I got out of my car, it quit raining. I found out later that not very long after I was safely in the store it was pelting rain again. I choose to believe that my God supplied my needs, my provisions, and my protection.

He often uses perfect timing as one of the ways that He watches over us. If I had missed one green light or been able to go just a little faster, I would not have had that parking place and that break in the weather! What a wonderful Father.

Prayer:

My Father, I know that You are a God of provision, purpose and plans. I thank You that You also answer my needs in practical terms. I pray that You will strengthen my belief to look for Your everyday blessings that I so often miss. I know that You have a greater purpose for everything and that I can trust You to fulfill Your plans for me. How I praise You! In Jesus' name, Amen.

Your Reflections:

Day 15

God is . . . Illuminating

Bible Reading: Acts 16:6-10

How does God illuminate our lives? He does it through the ministry of the Holy Spirit. When Jesus was taken up into heaven, He told His disciples that He would send the Comforter who is the Holy Spirit. He is the one who dwells within us whenever we receive Christ into our lives.

Any work that God does within us, He uses the Holy Spirit to reveal it to us. When we read Scripture, it is the Spirit's job to illuminate and bring it to our understanding. Whenever we feel "led" to do a particular spiritual thing, it is the Spirit revealing it to us.

Paul was greatly used by the Holy Spirit and was in tune to His urgings. His whole ministry was led or prevented by the Holy Spirit. "Paul and Silas traveled through the area of Phrygia and Galatia, because the Holy Spirit had prevented them from preaching in the province of Asia at that time . . . That night Paul had a vision: A man from Macedonia in northern Greece was standing there pleading with him. Come over to Macedonia and help us! So we decided to head for Macedonia at once, having concluded that God was calling us to preach the Good News there" Acts 16:6-9 (NLT).

In the early church, they were led mightily by the Holy Spirit. Do we get this kind of direction today? According to Acts 2:17, Paul wrote, "In the last days, God says, I will pour out my spirit on all people" (NIV). If we truly believe that, then we have to believe that He still leads our everyday lives today. We may not see such dramatic results for various reasons.

One reason is that we do not really open our hearts to accept what the Holy Spirit is capable of doing in and through us. When we begin to believe the fact that God, through the Holy Spirit, gives us direction and speaks to us, we begin to see it in our lives as well.

It is very subtle, and we have to be in tune with Him, but the Holy Spirit will lead us when we really listen and desire for Him to do so. Peter wrote, "Above all, you must realize that no prophecy in Scripture ever came from the prophet's own understanding or from human initiative. No, those prophets were moved by the Holy Spirit and they spoke from God" 2 Peter1:20-21 (NLT).

Personal Note:

I have found in my own journey that whenever I am really seeking God for direction there is a prodding within that is different from any other feeling or thought that I might have. I think that the closer I walk with my Father, the more I will understand His leading. Much of the time, when I am in my "busy mode" it is easy to overlook the gentle nudges. That is why I am trying so hard to listen intently to my Father, so that I will be able to hear the Holy Spirit when He desires to speak to me.

Someone referred to His guidance as that "sweet spot" which is deep inside my being. My heart's desire is to allow the "sweetness" to illuminate every area and become greater and greater so that my life might illuminate all that God is working within me.

Prayer:

Father, help me to understand with my heart when You are leading me. Illuminate me with Your presence, Lord. Thank You for Your love and mercy to me. In my Savior's precious name, Amen.

Your Reflections:

Day 16

God is . . . Visibly Invisible

Bible Reading: Colossians 1:15-20

One of the things that humanity has had problems with from the very beginning is how to believe when we cannot visually see God. We assume that because we cannot see Him that He does not exist. However, is that really an accurate assumption? Most of us are very good at camouflage. Few people really know what we are truly like inside. Moreover, we work hard at keeping up the façade.

God knew from the beginning that man would have a struggle believing in Him by faith alone.

God, after centuries of working with His chosen people and watching them fall deeper into sin, came to earth in the visible form of Jesus Christ. "Christ is the visible image of the invisible God. He existed before anything was created and is supreme over all creation" Colossians 1:16 (NLT).

Christ performed countless miracles and signs that He was the Son of God, nonetheless only a few believed Him. After His resurrection, however, He appeared to over 500 people and those 500 changed the course of history and the world.

Today, as a whole, we are more skeptical than ever. However, God has His chosen few, those of us who believe Him, who want His precious gift of salvation and who want to make Him Lord of our lives. In doing so, He dramatically changes our lives.

"And now, just as you accepted Christ Jesus as your Lord, you must continue to follow Him. Let your roots grow down into Him, and let your lives be built on Him. Then your faith will grow strong in the truth you were taught and you will overflow with thanksgiving" Colossians 2:6-7 (NLT). Our Father becomes very real to us whenever we allow His Son to build our lives on His firm foundation by faith in Him. The invisible becomes visible.

Personal Note:

I am glad that Christ chose me and I said "yes" to Him. This simple act allowed me to be one of the chosen few who are part of His family. As I grow in faith, God becomes increasingly real to me. Choosing to walk in God's ways without compromise may not be the easy path, but I would not change it for anything.

As I become stronger in the truth, God shines His light more and more on the areas of my life that still need to grow in His grace and mercy. However, every step of faith I take brings so much joy and peace that it is, at times, hard to contain. I know that as I trust and allow the Holy Spirit more freedom to work in my life, and listen more intently to His urging, the walls and the facades are breaking down and more of Christ is coming out.

The work that He does within me, the secret private things that no one can see, may at times be painful, but it is truly worth everything. We may not see God, but we can see the result of His work all around us and through us! My desire is for my life to display the invisible work of God so that it will be visible to others. How I praise Him!

Prayer:

Father, I thank You for revealing Yourself, to a greater extent, as I open up to You. I am grateful to You for breaking down the walls and mending the cracks of my life through the great gift of Your Son, Jesus Christ, my Lord and Savior. The invisible is truly becoming visible. Thank You. In His name, I pray this, Amen.

Your Reflections:

Day 17

God is . . . My Nerve Calmer

Bible Reading: Numbers 27:15-22

Moses had been an outstanding leader of the people and now it was time for him to turn over the command to someone else. I am sure there were many speculations, grumblings and wondering who would be their new leader. Who could possibly replace Moses? I imagine that nerves were running high as the people tried to envision who could capably take over this tremendous task.

It would have to be someone who was both goal-oriented and people-oriented. Moses did not want to leave this job unfinished. He wanted to be sure that whoever was going to be their new leader would be God's choice. He went to the One who had been his problem solver his whole life, God, who created every one.

As Moses talked to God, he said, "Give them someone who will guide them wherever they go and will lead them into battle, so the community of the Lord will not be like sheep without a shepherd. The Lord replied: Take Joshua son of Nun, who has the Spirit in him, and lay your hands on him . . . Transfer some of your authority to him so the whole community of Israel will obey him" Numbers 27:17, 18, 20 (NLT). This would allow the people to build confidence in their new leader and learn to take direction from him. Joshua was very much the right leader for that turbulent time in history. He was able to calm the nerves of the people and give them direction. God will always have someone whom He uses to calm our nerves as we walk through the rocky path of life.

Personal Note:

From my journal on November 16, 2000. "How appropriate it is to be in this spot in my devotional right at a time when our country is facing the closest election ever. Everything seems such a mess and the solutions seem to be along party lines. Only a God who is completely in charge of "His man for our times" can sort this out without dividing our country right down the middle. "O Father, please give me peace to trust You, knowing that You are in full control and that Your ultimate plan will be fulfilled. "

That certainly was a very tense and nervous time for our country! That election was particularly troubling. I could not seem to rest. I remember crying out to God and asking Him to give me His peace because I knew that there was such turmoil all around me. A tremendous calm came over me and I knew that God's choice would prevail, and there was no need for me to worry about it. Our country went through a very tough time in that election. I am still troubled by the hatred that seems to divide our country.

I pray that our nation will be able to start thinking more positively in the future and allowing God to calm us, because ultimately, He holds the whole world and all of its leaders in His hands. It does not matter whether I personally like the choice. I know I will sleep better if I can continue to rely on God for every decision. For my country, and for my life, He is my nerve calmer!

Prayer:

Father, we are drawing close to another election year. I pray for the President and for the other important positions that govern us. Help us to unite again as a country and return to being the United States of America. Help me to turn to You, calm my heart and give me peace. Have mercy on our nation and heal our land. In Jesus' name, Amen.

Your Reflections:

Day 18

God is . . . Divine Sovereignty

Bible Reading: Job 38:1-11

What is divine sovereignty? It is the very highest in command, independent of anyone or anything else, predominant in everything, self governing and limitless. It may be hard for mere mortals to comprehend such power but it is the nucleus of God.

One of the best illustrations of God's divine sovereignty is the story of Job. We remember how even Satan still had to report to God and was restrained from certain things for which God limited Him. Satan was allowed to bring about the most severe testing any human could endure, but God told him, you must not kill Job. After the trial was almost complete, Job finally asked God some questions and God told him directly and straightforwardly who was in command.

These two chapters in Job show that God is indeed "The Sovereign One," who can truly control everything. God speaks to Job, "Who is this that questions my wisdom? Brace yourself like a man, because I have some questions for you." God goes on to explain who He is. "Where were you when I laid the foundations of the earth? Tell me, if you know so much. Who determined its dimensions and stretched out the surveying line? What supports its foundations, and who laid its cornerstone as the morning stars sang together and all the angels shouted for joy?" Job 38:4-7 (NLT). God goes on to describe exactly how He created everything.

After such a stern correction, God completely restored Job and everything that he had. Job received more abundance than he had ever known. "So the Lord blessed Job in the second half of his life even more than in the beginning" Job 42:12 (NLT). That is our divinely sovereign God!

Personal Notes:

I admit that I have not always understood why God does some of the things He does, but it is not my place to question. He created me, along with everything else that exists. He could have been a real harsh dictator in all of His dealings with man, but what He is, more than anything, is love and He takes pleasure in bringing us joy.

Yes, He has rules. Yes, He is just. Nevertheless, with His justice is mercy, grace and a way to escape. In His righteousness, He must enforce judgment for disobedience to His rules. We who are His chosen ones, those who accept His great plan of salvation through His Son, will escape all of the wrath that God will pour out on the wicked and finally to Satan himself at the end of this age.

Our future, as His beloved children, is to live with this loving Father forever and ever. What He has prepared for us is beyond our wildest imaginations. In His sovereignty He will mete out whatever He has for us here on earth; and whether we understand it or not, it is His plan not ours. How thankful I am that He loves me and includes me as part of His kingdom. He loves each of us, equally! How I honor and adore Him!

Prayer:

O Father, You do exactly what pleases You, and You desire to love me and shower me with such a rich bounty of blessing that I cannot even begin to imagine it. I cannot fathom such deep love, which You delight in bestowing on me. How humble I feel in Your presence. How I praise and adore You. Thank You, in Your Son's wonderful name, the name of Jesus! Amen.

Your Reflections:

Day 19

God is . . . Sovereign Love

Bible Reading: Romans 8:35-39

How can I describe love? It is one of those things like faith and hope that you know you have, but you cannot verbally describe it. It can be an uplifting and passionate thing, or a destructive force in a life that is abused by it. Our human love seems to be something that we accept if we like it and reject if it is not going our way. Sovereign love is so different!

It is hard for us to understand a love so deep and so enduring that nothing can separate us from it. We may deeply love our spouses, our children, grandchildren and special friends, but there are times even in the best of relationships that we are disappointed, hurt, and less passionate about our love. Our love may not stop, but our feelings of love can be altered.

However, God's love for us is so deep and pure that He never goes by how He feels about loving us. He always loves us, even when we are not lovable. "And I am convinced that nothing can ever separate us from God's love. Neither death nor life, neither angels nor demons, neither our fears for today nor our worries about tomorrow—not even the powers of hell can separate us from God's love. No power in the sky above or in the earth below—indeed, nothing in all creation will ever be able to separate us from the love of God that is revealed in Christ Jesus our Lord" Romans 8:38-39 (NLT).

What an awesome truth! He knows every detail of our lives before we are even born. He knows the exact moment, generation and the right circumstances that will come into our lives. We exist to fulfill His divine purpose for us. Since God created us, He chooses whatever He wants for us. We may not understand His reasoning, but that is all part of our faith. We trust in knowing that His love is far above our comprehension. "The Lord does whatever pleases Him throughout all heaven and earth, and on the seas and in their depth" Psalm 135:6 (NLT).

Personal Note:

As I think about God's sovereign love, several things come to mind. He created me. The Bible says that it pleases Him to love me. In my finite mind, I use as an example, our pets. Whenever we get a kitten or a puppy, we make them part of our family. They are entirely at our mercy. I have two cats that we obtained when they were only about 6 weeks old.

Unlike God, I cannot read their future but there are certain things that I knew those kittens would be going through. Taking them to the veterinarian, spaying them, getting their shots, riding in our car—I knew they would not like it, but I also recognized that they must go through these things because it was best for them to grow up as happy healthy pets who are now a special part of our family.

When they first came home after all that surgery, they looked pathetic. Oh, how my heart went out to them. How I wished that it were not necessary for them to go through all that they did. Nevertheless, I had the overall picture. I knew that if these things were not done, much worse could come upon them.

We have a lot of wildlife around our home; and though most would not hurt them, we did not want them to face the dangers that lurked outside. Six years later, they are happy well-adjusted cats who have complete trust in us. That is how I view my Father's love for me.

I may not like going through whatever the trial, but He knows the total picture and the result. I believe that He hurts right along with me but He just wants me to trust Him. I am confident that He knows what is the very best for me. His love allows me to go through things, so that He can bring about His optimum purpose. What an awesome God!

Prayer:

Father, how I thank You for Your sovereign love that surpasses anything that I can imagine. I pray that You will help me to trust You when I go through deep waters. To know that You always do what is the best for me. Your love reaches to the depth of my soul! How I praise You and thank You! In Jesus' name, Amen.

Your Reflections:

Day 20

God is . . . Compassionate

Bible Reading: Psalm 145:8-12

Our God is all about compassion, boundless compassion! This was one of the first attributes that God demonstrated. What mercy He gave to Adam and Eve when they disobeyed His clear instructions.

He had given very specific commands to them. There was no doubt in their mind that they were not to eat of the tree of the knowledge of good and evil. Yet, they did it anyway. Why? A snake told Eve it would be good and she believed him! However, I believe it was much more complex than that.

Perhaps as they passed by that tree, day after day, and heard the serpents urgings, something deep inside started the thought process that maybe he was right. It became easier to yield to the temptation of the serpent when they stopped and thought about it a while. Once they sinned, the blame game began. God could have struck them dead on the spot, wiped the slate clean and started over, but He did not. His love and compassion allowed them to live.

God knew that this act of sin changed everything! Man, whom He created in His image would not be able to resist sin on his own. God would need to make the ultimate sacrifice so that you and I could be a part of His eternal kingdom, so He sent His Son to earth to atone for all our sins.

One of the most evident qualities of Christ was compassion. His love and compassion were the biggest part of His ministry. He healed the sick, raised the dead and wept over His friend. He called the little children to Him and came to the aid of the poor and downtrodden. He wept over Jerusalem, because He knew that His own people would put Him to death. He was the Son of God! He was just being who He is! "The Lord is merciful and compassionate, slow to get angry and filled with unfailing love" Psalm 145:8 (NLT).

His most compassionate act was yet to come when He carried all of our sin and iniquity; and the Father had to turn His back on His own Son because a righteous and holy God cannot look upon sin. I Peter 2:24 reads, "Who Himself bore our sins in His own body on the tree, that we, having died to sins, might live for righteousness—by whose stripes you were healed" (NKJ). What great compassion and love!

Personal Note:

Compassion is something that God has bestowed on me countless times. This attribute is a vital part of His love and mercy. No matter how often I fail Him, He is always waiting with love and compassion to bring me back into relationship with Him. When I falter, He picks me up and carries me. "The Lord is like a Father to His children, tender and compassionate to those who fear Him. For He knows how weak we are, He remembers we are only dust" Psalm 103:13-14 (NLT). My Father treats me with tenderness and consideration . . . and I am so thankful that He does!

Prayer:

Father, Your compassion is beyond my comprehension! How I appreciate Your tender loving care. You reach down and treat me with so much love and understanding that my heart sings with joy because of You. I thank You. In Jesus' name, Amen.

Your Reflections:

Day 21

God is . . . Our Sanctuary

Bible Reading: Psalm 73:21-28

Asaph was a great musician who was given the honor to play his instruments for King David. He was a Levite—their job was to minister in the temple. Asaph played a lyre before the Ark of the Covenant. His life as well as his talent had to be pure before God for such an important job. He also was honored by God to write 12 wonderful psalms. In Psalm 73, we read of Asaph's struggle to try to understand why God allowed the wicked to prosper. He wrote, "Look at these wicked people—enjoying a life of ease while their riches multiply" Psalm 73:12 (NLT).

Don't we at times feel the same way today? God gave Asaph a good viewpoint as he learned to trust God's ways he wrote, "I tried to understand why the wicked prosper but what a difficult task it is! Then I went into Your sanctuary, O God, and I finally understood the destiny of the wicked" Psalm 73:16 (NLT).

Going into God's sanctuary, what does that mean? Asaph is not talking about going into a building to find his answers. He went into the sanctuary to pray seeking God's viewpoint and learning His ways.

When we come before God to seek His ways He restores our souls as well. He loves us to open our hearts and allow His presence to enter into our lives and teach us. When we are in distress and cannot comprehend why something is happening, God will be our sanctuary and many things will become clear.

In the very last verse of this psalm, Asaph is finally freed from his unrest. "But as for me, how good it is to be near God! I have made the Sovereign Lord my shelter, and I will tell everybody about the wonderful things You do!" Psalm 73:28 (NLT). What a peace Asaph found when he visited God's sanctuary! We can experience that same peace when we come into God's presence and let Him restore our souls!

Personal Note:

Worry or distress is never the right answer. My spirit is always troubled if I start worrying about what someone else might have or think, instead of concentrating on my own blessings. It is only when I am willing to release the problem into my heavenly Father's capable hands, that He gives me peace.

Sometimes He even chides me by letting me know that I was fretting over something that really was not my business, but His! He is the Sovereign God who made all things and knows about all things. In Psalm 73:21 Asaph wrote, "Then I realized that my heart was bitter, and I was all torn up inside" (NLT). This can be a real struggle for me, at times, but God will meet me wherever I am hurting, lovingly correct me, restore, and calm my anxious heart. He is my Sanctuary!

Prayer:

Father, help me not to worry about someone else's life, which is safely in Your hands. Instead, help us to bring that person before You in prayer and completely turn them over to You, so that I may experience Your healing restoration. In Jesus' name, Amen.

Your Reflections:

Day 22

God is . . . Merciful

Bible Reading: Lamentations 3:18-27

Jeremiah the prophet wrote "The Book of Lamentations." He is called the "weeping prophet" because he agonized over the way his beloved country, Judah, was ignoring his message of doom and ignoring their God. No matter how bad it got, Jeremiah remained faithful to God. He probably went through more trials in his life than most people, yet he remained faithful and called his God merciful. He was thrown in prison and then into a cistern and was stripped of all earthly wealth. No one ever believed his prophecies or took him seriously, he was rejected by his people, yet he remained obedient.

In today's reading, we get a glimpse of Jeremiah's attitude. "The thought of my suffering and homelessness is bitter beyond words. I will never forget this awful time as I grieve over my loss. Yet I still dare to hope when I remember this: The faithful love of the Lord never ends! His mercies never cease" Lamentations 3:19-21 (NLT). WOW! Would we have been so confident if we had gone through everything that he did?

Too often, I complain and rely on people's sympathy because of what I am going through. I can become full of a "poor-me" attitude. However, Jeremiah is an awesome example of his reliance on his God and not on people.

I know my God is loving, kind, and merciful to me, even though I go through some very deep waters at times. It is such comfort to remember when I am discouraged that like Jeremiah I can trust my heavenly Father. He wrote. "Great is His faithfulness; His mercies begin afresh each morning." Lamentations 3:23 (NLT), What a wonderful verse! Every day is a new day. We can lift up our heads and proclaim that God is faithful, and His mercy is just enough to get through today!

Personal Note:

No matter how bad things are around me, I serve a God whose mercies begin afresh each morning. All I need to do is to trust Him today and ask Him to help me get through the deep waters today.

How easy at times to forget that! When I start my day with a special communing with Him in the morning, things go a lot smoother. If I rush through my time with Him, it is easier to let situations around me influence me. "The Lord is good to those who depend on Him, to those who search for Him. So it is good to wait quietly for salvation from the Lord" Lamentations 3:25-26 (NLT). It is in the quietness that I receive the most blessing from my Father. May I learn to be faithful to this quietness and receive His mercy afresh each morning!

Prayer:

Oh Father, help me to be obedient to You. You are a merciful God, who judges me through the blood of Your Son instead of looking at my sinfulness. I praise You for Your faithfulness. In Jesus' Name, Amen.

Your Reflections:

Day 23

God is . . . Our Thought Bank

Bible Reading: Philippians 4:8-13

What is in your thought bank? We all have them. It is what happens just beneath the surface of our conscious mind. Thoughts run through our mind constantly, both negative and positive. When we feed our thoughts negative messages, such as: "I cannot do this,' 'I am not good enough,' or 'who would ever want me?'" We become sad and depressed.

Many times our negative thoughts are baggage that we have been carrying all our lives. They influence how we respond to different situations and even how we respond to each other. They also affect how we interpret what someone else says to us. For example, "You look so great today!" That is probably a real compliment, but we may hear it as, Wow! I wonder how I usually look!

God wants to give us a positive mind set, so that our thought bank is full of His confidence and goodness. When we are full of His perception and realize that He made each of us unique, we can move forward and have the negative thoughts changed to positive ones.

Using the example above, when God fills our lives and thoughts and someone tells us, "You look so great today;" our reasoning will soar and say thank you with a big smile on our face, because we know that God is shining through our life today. Philippians 4:11b-13 reads, ". . . for I have learned how to be content with whatever I have. I know how to live on almost nothing or with everything, I have learned the secret of living in every situation, whether it is with a full stomach or empty, with plenty or little. For I can do everything through Christ, who gives me strength" (NLT). Paul was a positive thinker even though he had many trials because he trusted God to fill his thought bank with God's assessment! What an amazing example he was to us!

Personal Note:

I was chastened the other day by a positive comment a friend made. I went to a celebration of her birthday and she looked at me and said, "I haven't seen you in a while and look at you, you are walking better than ever." Then she turned to another friend whom I did not know and said, "This woman has a remarkable story of how she was in a wheelchair and homebound. She then trusted God and He healed her!"

I then had the opportunity to tell this woman my story. God had miraculously healed my knee which had been through two surgeries, the last not being a success and I was in a wheelchair most of the time and unable to walk without pain and I was no longer able to drive. Today, I get along without support or pain and drive anywhere I want to go!

It was not until later that I remembered how much I had been complaining in front of these same people about having a breathing problem and not being able to get enough air.

I have been struggling right now with breathing and shortness of breath for several weeks. Doctors are trying to find the cause of it. I have been going through some cardiac tests and the unknown is always a challenge; but by talking about it in front of those who knew about my other healing, God showed me that I cancelled some of the blessing He had for them because of my negative attitude on this issue.

I repented to Him but I missed a great opportunity because I chose to have unconstructive words instead of God's constructive ones. How often have I missed being a blessing to someone because of my unenthusiastic responses instead of God's optimistic ones? How I want to be more diligent in seeking God's thoughts so I may store up positive words from God's thought bank.

Prayer:

Oh Father, how I long to hear Your voice and Your thoughts within me. Help me to listen more attentively to You as You continue to guide my thinking and my actions. In the mighty name of Jesus, Amen.

Your Reflections:

Day 24

God is . . . A Request Acknowledger

Bible Reading: Genesis 19:16-29

When my children were growing up, it was always so much fun to fill their requests, especially at Christmas. I would shop and then try to hide the gifts until the big day came around. The best part was seeing their shining faces as they happily opened each present and found their request had been granted.

God loves to shower favor on us whenever we are obedient to Him. It brings to my mind the story of Lot, Abraham's nephew. Lot had been given the chance to choose the part of the land that He wished to inherit, by his uncle Abraham. Lot had chosen what he thought was the prime land and Abraham had taken the more desolate share. Nevertheless, God blessed Abraham and the land, which God gave him for an inheritance and continued to pour out His blessing on him.

God loved Abraham so much that He decided to bring him in on the decision that He had already made, to destroy the city that Lot had chosen. Sodom was so vile that when two angels came to visit Lot to tell him to flee, the men of the city tried to break down the door to get at the angels so that they could commit immoral acts with them. Lot was so scared that he offered his own two daughters who were virgins for the men to use anyway they wished. Can you even imagine doing that?

Long story short, God saved Lot and his family. Even with all of the immorality, the angels still had to drag Lot and his family to safety.

"When Lot still hesitated, the angels seized his hand and the hands of his wife and two daughters and rushed them to safety outside the city" Genesis 19:19 (NLT).

In spite of Lot's reluctance, I believe that God honored Abraham's obedience before He destroyed Sodom. Because Abraham had requested that Lot be saved, God favored him and answered his request. Verse 29 reads, "But God had listened to Abraham's request and kept Lot safe, removing him from the disaster that engulfed the cities on the plain" (NLT). Because of Abraham's faithful obedience, Lot and his two daughters had been saved! God rewards faithfulness!

Personal Note:

I cannot help but wonder how many things God has favored me with because of my obedience. On the other hand, how many things have not gone well because of my disobedience? Nevertheless, God is very merciful. He, by His grace, has forgiven me of my waywardness. My heart's desire is to trust Him one day at a time and live in obedience just one day at a time. I know when I do, He will shower down blessing and favor upon me. He will acknowledge my requests according to His purpose when I remain faithful to Him!

Prayer:

Dear Father, thank You for the favor that You provide each day. Help me to seek Your best so that I will live according to Your plan for me. I know that You hear my request and answer according to Your purpose. I praise You for Your sovereignty! In Jesus' precious name, Amen.

Your Reflections:

Day 25

God is . . . Present Everywhere

Bible Reading: Psalm 139:7-12

God's presence is everywhere! I have heard this expression most of my life, but I am not sure that I really had a clear picture of how this can be. My finite mind cannot grasp such a wondrous fact. How can He be in me and with me and yet be with someone in Australia at the same time. I really had never thought about it that much, it was just a fact that I accepted, because the Bible said so.

When we read this familiar Psalm, it makes it very plain that God indeed is everywhere we go—we cannot hide anywhere from God. "Where can I go from Your Spirit? Where can I flee from Your presence? If I go up to the heavens, You are there; if I make my bed 'in the depths' You are there. If I rise on the wings of the dawn, if I settle on the far side of the sea, even there Your hand will guide me, Your right hand will hold me fast" Psalm 139:7-10 (NIV).

Recently, I found an analogy that represented how this might work. I started picturing it in my mind and came up with this example. We cannot see the air that we breathe, yet we accept that no matter where we are, it will be there for our next breath. It was such a blessing for me to picture God's presence in the same way. He is as present as the air I breathe.

I often go to bed at night and in the darkness feel His presence. "If I say, surely the darkness will hide me and the light become night around me, even the darkness will not be dark to You; the night will shine like the day, for darkness is as light to You" Psalm 139:11-12

(NIV). What a wonderful way to go to sleep realizing God's presence surrounds me!

Personal Note:

When I first started to think of God's presence, I was in my peaceful living room which I was drawn to use as my prayer room. I had my eyes closed and was praying earnestly and praising God. I was silent, and as the silence engulfed me, it was as a cool breeze rested on my face. A very gentle breeze, but I felt God's presence surrounding me. I knew it immediately. Just like I know the air is all around me and available to me. It is such a blessing to know how near God is. I have to receive His presence, just as I receive air. I know without a shadow of a doubt that He is always available. Just as close as the air I breathe! That was the beginning of an intimacy with my heavenly Father that I cherish every day. How I love this matchless God!

Prayer:

Father, oh, how I love You! How thankful I am that You are always available to me, just like the air I breathe. Your presence surrounds me and keeps me safe. I know that Your right hand will hold me fast, through all of the valleys of life as well as the mountaintops! How I praise You! In Jesus' name, Amen.

Your Reflections:

Day 26

God is . . . Consistent

Bible Reading: Psalm 102:23-28

One thing that brings me great comfort in my walk with the Lord is that He is always consistent. Whatever He says, He will do! He never gets off the path or distracted in His dealings with me. He is like following the double line on my highway of life. I know that no one will hit me head-on because He has that double line there to protect me. I am very safe when I consistently follow His purpose for me.

It is easy, however, to get off the path and become distracted. When I do, I can always turn back to the God who remains consistent forever. "But You are always the same; You will live forever. The children of Your people will live in security. Their children's children will thrive in Your presence" Psalm 102:27-28 (NIV).

I love the fact that when we become part of God's family we have great peace and security available to us. Often we forget, and worry or fret about things, which we should just turn over to our consistent God.

When we are rebellious, He is still there just waiting for us to ask His forgiveness and come back to the safety of His steadfastness. The Bible is full of examples. The children of Israel went away from Him time after time, but He always allowed them to come back. Many times, however, they had to endure strict judgment because of their unbelief.

He disciplines us when we go astray as well, but when we learn to endure His testing and discipline there is great reward. "For you know that when your faith is tested, your endurance has a chance to grow. So let it grow, for when your endurance is fully developed, you will be perfect and complete, needing nothing" James 1:3-4 (NLT).

Personal Note:

Consistency—I still have a long way to go on this one! I am fine for a while and then it seems like all of a sudden BAM! I am on the wrong side of the double line. Life hits and hits hard!

I have grown quite a bit in this area and am less inconsistent now. I come back to Him sooner and I do not fret and worry as much. Nevertheless, I have a long way to go before I reach the perfection the apostle James mentioned.

I seem to hit plateaus where my mind becomes scattered instead of focused on Him. I hate that feeling, so I usually get on my knees in prayer to ask His forgiveness and for Him to bring my mind into focus on Him again. Sometimes it takes a while to get that all cleared up in my life. I am never comfortable, however, when I lose track of the center of His direction and guidance.

Prayer:

Father, thank You for being a consistent source in my life. I know that when I keep my heart focused on You, that You will never let me down. Lord, help me to keep You as the center in my life. In Christ's name I pray, Amen.

Your Reflections:

Day 27

God is . . . Praiseworthy

Bible Reading: 2 Chronicles 5:1-14

Praise is something that God dearly loves and it excites Him. In this passage, Solomon had just completed the building of the Temple of God—the first permanent house He ever had. "Then the priests carried the Ark of the Lord's Covenant into the inner sanctuary of the Temple—the Most Holy Place—and placed it beneath the wings of the cherubim. The cherubim spread their wings over the Ark, forming a canopy over the Ark and its carrying poles" 2 Chronicles 5:7-8 (NLT).

What a spectacular picture this brings to mind as I try to imagine how God must have felt when His precious Ark of the Covenant finally had a permanent home. I can envision His eyes being glued to the spot as His people were finally able to give Him the respect that He had waited patiently for throughout all of the generations before them. It was quite a ceremony! The priests purified themselves along with the Levites who were musicians. With reverence and awe, they sang to the Lord with accompaniment of instruments. They lifted their music heavenward with thanksgiving and praise to the God who had brought them through so much. Now He had a permanent home to dwell in!

At that incredible instant in history, God made His appearance. "At that moment a thick cloud filled the Temple of the Lord. The priests could not continue their service because of the cloud, for the glorious presence of the Lord filled the Temple of God!" 2 Chronicles 5:14 (NLT). "Then Solomon prayed, O Lord, You have said that You would live in a thick cloud of darkness. Now I have built a glorious Temple for You, a place where You can live forever!" 2 Chronicles 6:1-2 (NLT). Solomon went on to praise and honor the God who had been so good to him. This chapter brings to life this spectacular event! How beautifully Solomon brought praise to our praiseworthy God!

Personal Note:

I cannot picture how it must have felt for those who were in the Temple that day! However, God is the same today as He was then. He adores praise! The psalms are full of them and all through Scripture, praise and worship flow like a fine silk thread weaving its way through book after book and clear to the end of Revelation!

As I learn more about my Father, one thing remains very consistent on its own—praise! True praise brings me to my knees in humble adoration to the God who knew me before the foundations of the earth. He formed me in my mother's womb to be here at this exact moment in time.

Praise also keeps my attitude positive. I cannot think about anything negative and praise Him at the same time. It flows smoothly throughout my day, no matter what the circumstance. Even when it is hard to do, God tells us to offer unto Him a sacrifice of praise! There are times that the only way to get through a situation is to praise and thank my Father for the blessings He has given me. Oh, may I always remember to offer up adoration to Him often throughout my daily life!

Prayer:

Father, how wonderful You are! You who made the heavens and the earth and formed everything that is in it. How I praise You for Your unfailing love. I come before Your holiness and realize that without the covering of Jesus, I could not freely come to You

and have a relationship with You. How thankful I am that You care so much about me! You are truly worthy to be praised. In Jesus' Name, Amen.

Your Reflections:

Day 28

God is . . . Our Triumph

Bible Reading: I Thessalonians 5:12-24

When we moved to Oregon, I discovered what real triumph was. We have two Universities that are only about 35 miles apart and the competition between them in football is a delight to watch.

Our daughter-in-law went to Oregon State University and oh, what joy it is for us when they win, especially over the University of Oregon! However, what I learned from her is that her beloved team does not have to win the game to win her heart. OSU is not always the best team, but if they score more points than they did last week, it is a victory for all. What a marvelous example this is of how we triumph in God. We will never be perfect but if we can reach new goals in Christ, we are victorious.

Just as football has rules to follow, God has set down some rules for us. Paul gave us one of the most concise instructions of any of the letters that he wrote. Writing some of the shortest verses in the Bible, he advises us on how to be a triumphant Christian. He does not waste a single word. "Be joyful always; pray continually; give thanks in all circumstances, for this is God's will for you in Christ Jesus" I Thessalonians 5:16-18 (NIV). Three verses and twenty words! How powerful, yet challenging to accomplish!

"Be joyful always." We can only triumph, however, when we let go of our circumstance and allow God to take over. When we see God in everything, He gives us power to be joyful as He brings us through the trial and safely to the other side. It is not an easy or natural thing for us. We like to control things. Nevertheless, triumph is available to us.

"Pray continually!" Give thanks in all circumstances. What He does is take a bad situation and bring about His good through it. God is not a God of any evil; nonetheless, He will allow it to bring about His greater good. "But you belong to God my dear children; you have already won a victory over those people because the spirit who lives in you is greater than the spirit who lives in the world" I John 4:4 (NLT). He alone will make us triumph over all circumstances!

Personal Note:

Satan reigns here on earth and his purpose is to keep us defeated. If he can do that, he accomplishes his goal. However, Satan cannot throw any of his arrows unless God permits it. God's permissive will is very difficult for us to understand, but I try to explain it to a degree through the raising of my own children.

I remember our daughter Jill riding her bike. I would warn her repeatedly not to ride her bike down the hill. One day, she decided to do it anyway. We ended up in the emergency room with a smashed face, a split chin that still shows the scar from that fall and a concussion, arms and legs bruised and beaten and a miserable time ahead of her. Did I take her up that hill and make her go down it to her sorrow? Of course not! Did I know that she would come to harm by riding her bicycle? Yes, because I knew her personality! However, did we love her and nurse her back to health and did she learn a huge lesson? Yes!

Sometimes my human nature overrides God's purpose. When it does, God will say, "OK, Satan, give her just a little rope, not enough to hang herself but just enough to test her." Often our human nature is the vehicle used to trap us in our own self-centeredness.

Some of those tests are so painful for me that at times, I do not know if I can stand anymore. Nevertheless, I am a child of the King and God will always bring His goodness out of bad circumstances. Therefore, I can be thankful in all circumstances. He has everything in His control! It gives me such a sense of stability to know that Satan cannot ever use anything that God cannot take and turn to His good so I can be triumphant in my walk with Him.

Prayer:

Father, it is hard sometimes to understand Your will, but I know that You always cause me to triumph over sin if I just put my trust in You. You bring forth the greater good in my life, even when things look bleak! I know that You are my victory! In Jesus' Name, Amen.

Your Reflections:

Day 29

God is . . . The Last Word

Bible Reading: Psalm 37:16-24

We are living in a time that violence and corruption surround us on every side. Terrorism is rampant and new evil forces are rising to the forefront all of the time. No country on earth can feel confident that they will not be attacked by an evil force.

The Bible clearly talks about these same issues all throughout Scripture. That is because, by nature, we are evil. Left to our own devices, we are corrupt. My mother used to have a saying whenever she was talking about evil. She would say, "We cannot understand or condone their sin, but we need to remember that they do not know Christ so they are acting normal for them."

Without Christ, sinfulness is the norm, not the exception. Paul wrote, "Yes, they knew God, but they wouldn't worship Him as God or even give Him thanks. Moreover, they began to think up foolish ideas of what God was like. As a result, their minds became dark and confused. Claiming to be wise, they instead became utter fools . . . . They traded the truth about God for a lie. So they worshiped and served the things God created instead of the Creator Himself, Who is worthy of eternal praise! Amen" Romans 1:21, 22, 25 (NLT). We see this every day in our own country as well as around the world.

God knows exactly what is happening and who will seek after Him and who will not. His knowledge is not just individual but He governs our nations as well. God is in absolute control over all things and His goodness will prevail in the end! David wrote, "For the strength of the wicked will be shattered, but the Lord takes care of the godly" Psalm 37:17 (NLT). I am so thankful that I serve a God who has everything completely at His command. He will have the last word!

Personal Note:

It is very easy, at times, when I am conversing with another person, to want to have the last word. Especially if I am trying to make a point or wanting to share a thought.

I am learning however that it is a greater comfort to me to know that I can trust my God to be in charge not only of my life, but in the outcome of nations. They rise and fall by His Word, the evil and the good. Things may be scary out there, and I may not be alive when Jesus comes back for His bride, but I am confident that it will happen. I believe it will be soon and I hope I am living. What an awesome event it will be when all His chosen ones are called up to meet our Lord in the air! That will definitely be the final word!

Prayer:

O Father, how thankful I am that You control everything. I can count on You, knowing that no matter how bad things may look, Your goodness will reign forever and forever. I trust You! I know that You alone have the last word! In Jesus' powerful name, Amen.

Your Reflections:

Day 30

God is . . . A Healthy Prescription

Bible Reading: Matthew 5:1-12

The Beatitudes, as we call them, were at the very beginning of Jesus' Sermon on the Mount where He preached to thousands of people. I believe that by following these words of our Lord, we would have a very healthy spirit. I love how "The New Living Translation" frames this. Scripture.

(3.)   "God blesses those who are poor and realize their need for Him".

(4.)   "God blesses those who mourn, for they will be comforted."

(5.)   "God blesses those who are humble, for they will inherit the whole earth."

(6.)   "God blesses those who hunger and thirst for justice, for they will be satisfied."

(7.)   "God blesses those who are merciful, for they will be shown mercy."

(8.)   "God blesses those whose hearts are pure for they will see God."

(9.)   "God blesses those who work for peace for they will be called the children of God."

(10.) "God blesses those who are persecuted for doing right, for the kingdom of heaven is theirs."

(11.) "God blesses you when people mock you and persecute you and lie about you and say all sorts of evil things against you because you are my followers."

(12.) "Be happy about it! Be very glad! For a great reward awaits you in heaven. And remember, the ancient prophets were persecuted in the same way." Matthew 5:3-12

If we follow these principles, we will have consistent peace and joy. The stresses of life will not be able to affect us! Paul wrote, "Don't worry about anything; tell God what you need and thank Him for what He has done. Then you will experience God's peace, which exceeds anything we can understand. His peace will guard your hearts and minds as you live in Christ Jesus" Philippians 4:6-7 (NLT). Not an easy prescription, nevertheless, it is the greatest prescription of all!

Personal Note:

From my journal on December 11, 2000. The Beatitudes would give us a healthy and happy life, if we followed them. They are God's prescription for living."

In our culture today, we need only go to a bookstore or library and we can get self-help books on any subject. We pour billions of dollars a year into books on self-improvement, marriage relationships and other helps to improve our lives. I have bought my share as well!

Prescriptions for stress, depression, anxiety and sleep aids fill our medicine cabinets. However, if we would just apply the principles that Christ taught us to our lives, a healthy prescription would be our reward. The Beatitudes spoke to me in a completely new way. I am going to type them up in different translations and read them each morning as part of my devotional time. I know that when I do, God will reward me with the healthy life He has planned for me!

Prayer:

Father, thank You for showing me this gem of a passage of Scripture in a new light. Please help me to apply it to my own life as I continue to learn of You. You are the answer to our health when we learn to trust in You. Thanks You, In Jesus' name, Amen.

Your Reflections:

Day 31

God is . . . My Blueprint for Living

Bible Reading: Matthew 22:34-40

God has given us so many Scriptures to guide our lives as we learn to walk with Him. The Sermon on the Mount, which we find recorded in Matthew chapters five, six and seven, outlines the best blueprint for having a successful and contented life. It is a bright jewel, which talks about many problems that we face and Christ's solutions for them. It is very practical.

As I read this passage of Scripture I pondered what would be the summation of this precious jewel, I remembered how clearly Jesus answered the Pharisees when they asked Him what the greatest commandment was. Jesus answers, "Love the Lord your God with all your heart and all your soul and all your mind. This is the first and most important command. And the second is like the first; Love your neighbor as you love yourself. All the law and the writings of the prophets depend on these two commands" Matthew 22:37-40 (NCV).

When we get to the place that we can love in this way, all of the problems that Jesus dealt with in the Sermon on the Mount will automatically fall into place. We often quote "the golden rule." "Do unto others as you would have them do unto you" Luke 6:31 (NIV). This verse sums up how Jesus lived and how I should love Him. The closer I get to being able to love like Christ, the sooner I will develop into who God made me to be. This is His ultimate blueprint for us!

Personal Note:

What does it mean to love God with all my heart, soul and mind? It is reaching for perfection, as Jesus was the perfect image of the Father. I will never achieve that while I live here on earth, but every time I obey Him and give Him another area of my heart, soul and mind, I become a bit closer to His perfection.

It is a blessing to share some of my lessons, as an older adult, with the younger generation. The Bible tells us the young should learn from the old. I remember when I was a little girl. I would sit at my grandmother's feet and just listen to her tell stories of her childhood days. Her life was so much different from mine! She lived in the age of horse-drawn wagons and houses built just of boards hewn from trees that they cut down themselves and formed into boards.

My grandmother could do just about anything! At least to my young mind that is how it seemed. I thought she was about the best human being I had ever met. I never remember her getting angry with me. She seemed always patient and loving and she would keep showing me over and over how to do something.

I recall the time she taught me to crochet a doily. I was about ten years old. I labored over that doily and ripped out more than I completed; but when it was done, I was so proud that I had finished it. I ran and showed it to Grandma. She carefully examined it and then proceeded to rip it out! You see, there was a mistake back near the beginning! How painful it was for me to start that doily over again. I have never enjoyed crocheting to this day.

My heavenly Father is not like that. As I strive for His perfection, He has already forgiven me the mistake way back in the beginning and I start fresh every time I come to Him with a repentant heart. He wants me to continue growing in Him. He will erase every mistake as I reach upward and follow His blueprint for my life! What a wonderful Father I serve!

Prayer:

Father, how grateful I am that You gave me such a clear blueprint to follow. Thank You for Your everlasting patience as I learn

to love You with all my heart, soul and mind. Keep me always reaching toward Your high calling for my life. In Jesus' name, Amen.

Your Reflections:

Day 32

God is . . . The Creator of a Right Attitude

Bible Reading: Romans 13:6-14

From my journal on December 17, 2000, "A good attitude does more for my mental health and physical well-being than anything else. As I awaken to a new day each morning, a choice awaits me. What kind of an attitude will I have today? I know by experience that the days that I choose to be positive when I first get up; are much better days. Why I do not always choose this path is beyond me."

There are optimistic rules and goals that God has laid down for us to achieve as we are walking along His pathway. Paul wrote, "The night is almost gone; the day of salvation will soon be here. So remove your dark deeds like dirty clothes, and put on the shining armor of right living . . . Instead, clothe yourself with the presence of the Lord Jesus Christ. And don't let yourself think about ways to indulge your evil desires" Romans 13:12, 14 (NLT).

We can never be effective for Him if we have one foot in our fleshly desires and the other foot in our spiritual lives. Yet this is where many of us live. God does not like it when we are indecisive. He wants us to either live for Him or not. James wrote, "But when you ask Him, be sure that your faith is in God alone. Do not waiver, for a person with divided loyalties is as unsettled as a wave of the sea that is blown and tossed by the wind. Such people should not expect to receive anything from the Lord" James 1:6-7 (NLT).

What He desires most for us, is to love each other the way He loves us. Too often, we spend more time on talking negatively about someone and too little time seeking God's love and a righteous attitude within ourselves. Paul tells us, "Love does no wrong to others, so love fulfills the requirements of God's law" Romans 13:10 (NLT). He wants us to be careful to seek Him and His deepening love. When we do, we will have the "right attitude!"

Personal Note:

In the past few years, I have learned to start my day with my Lord. Reading His Word and a time of prayer are necessary for me. If I start doing other things before I carry out this act, my mind is scattered and I am out of sync. When I have a full calendar, it is tempting to shorten my time with Him. When I do, I am the one who is shortchanged. I feel more confident, I have a better attitude, the pressures of life do not affect me as much, and I am sure that I am much. more pleasant to be around when I start the day with my Lord. The deeper I walk with Him, the more I find it necessary and fruitful to be in His presence. He alone can give me a "right-living" attitude!

Prayer:

Father, thank You for Your desire to spend time with me. I cherish the moments of Your presence in my life. You fill me with Your love and help me get through the day. Thank You for helping my mind to focus on Your right attitude and Your amazing love. In Jesus' name, Amen.

Your Reflections:

Day 33

God is . . . Full of Unspeakable Joy

Bible Reading: Psalm 16:7-11

One of the things God blesses us with is His joy! Everything that He does is for His enjoyment and pleasure. Joy is another magnificent quality of God. However, sometimes it is hard for us to be full of joy! Too often, our thoughts are on negative things and we do not experience God's immeasurable joy. The more of our lives that we turn over to Him, the more joy we will experience.

When I first came to know Jesus and knew His forgiveness of my sin, I felt a great relief and an indescribable joy, because now I was ushered into the very family of God. "Though you have not seen Him, you love Him; and even though you do not see Him now, you believe in Him and are filled with an inexpressible and glorious joy, for you are receiving the goal of your faith, the salvation of your soul" I Peter 1:8 (NIV).

Somewhere along the way, we can lose our joy. We let life's trials and situations steal it from us. Nevertheless, God has promised us joy. "You have made known to me the path of life; You will fill me with joy in Your presence, with eternal pleasures at Your right hand" Psalm 16:11 (NIV). When God makes a promise to us, in most cases, there is something required of us in return. We have to be filled with His presence to experience full joy. Only when we utterly turn our lives over to Him, can we experience the kind of joy that He has available. What a marvelous gift He gives us when we are full of His joy!

Personal Note:

To receive all of God's joy I need to choose it daily. It is easy to let the cares and concerns of life sneak in and rob me of my joy. My goal is to press toward this mark as I start each day with Him. When I am in the fullness of His joy, my focus is on Him and nothing can distract me from it. I live each day with whatever situation arises, but deep inside His peace and joy are going to keep me grounded in Him.

In recent years, I have experienced great joy even amidst deep sorrow. This might sound inconsistent, but my Lord fills me with His joy no matter what the situation if I allow Him to do so. This is nothing that I can do for myself. It is supernatural! Only my Father can keep me so focused that I am not distracted from His joy! I thank Him with all of my heart for this amazing gift, which is always available to me. This is where I want to live, In His fullness, in His unspeakable joy!

Prayer:

Father, I pray each day as I am in Your presence that Your joy may flow freely into my inner being, as I learn to trust You in yet another area of my life. Fill me with Your overflowing joy! Just enough for today! That is all I need! In Jesus' name, Amen.

Your Reflections:

Day 34

God is . . . Selective

Bible Reading: Genesis 4:1-7

In the beginning of time, what made God choose Abel over Cain? They were the children of the first man and woman, Adam and Eve. Their mother and father must have told them about what it meant to sin and how glorious their lives were before they chose to eat the fruit of the tree of the knowledge of good and evil. As a parent, I cannot even fathom how they would not have been told all about sin and how to sacrifice unto God.

Cain was even the firstborn. Throughout the history of the generations in the Bible, it was a practice set down by God to honor the firstborn. There were a few exceptions. So why did God, right from the start, decide to accept Abel's offering and not Cain's?

I like how the New Century Version translates it. "Later, Cain brought some food from the ground as a gift to God. Abel brought the best parts from some of the firstborn of his flock. The Lord accepted Abel and his gift, but He did not accept Cain and his gift. So Cain became very angry and felt rejected" Genesis 4:3. The issue was not over meat versus vegetables, it was over the attitude of the giver and the preciousness of the gift. Cain just brought "some food" from the ground, not a lot of heart in it. However, Abel gave of his best, sacrificially.

How often have we given something to the Lord as a gift, but our heart has not been in it. Maybe we have asked Him for something that we want rather than giving Him the best that we have. God always honors sacrifice. When we come to Him, do we bring a sacrifice to Him?

One way to please Him is to bring a sacrifice of praise. Paul talks about this in Hebrews 13:15-16 "Through Jesus, therefore, let us continually offer to God a sacrifice of praise—the fruit of lips that confess His name. And do not forget to do good and to share with others, for with such sacrifices God is pleased" (NIV). Yes, God is selective! If I want to please Him and find favor with Him, I need to give Him a sacrifice of praise, especially when I do not feel like it! That is what sacrifice is all about!

Personal Note:

When I am in prayer with Him, some mornings I just do not feel like starting my day yet. I am sleepy and can hardly keep my eyes open. Nevertheless, when I start praising Him and telling Him how precious He is to me and how magnificent He is, the next thing I know, I am not sleepy anymore. I am filled with His joy and ready to open up for Him to fill me with His presence. The blessing flows full and free and my day is off to an awesome start!

Prayer:

Father, How grateful I am that You are not selective in Your favor. Help me to continue to learn how to please You and how to praise You. Refresh me every morning as I learn to honor and obey You, one day at a time. In Jesus' Name, Amen.

Your Reflections:

Day 35

God is . . . Sovereign Beyond Understanding

Bible Reading: Romans 9:14-26

When we are reading about the sovereignty of God, it is difficult to understand. Today's reading is a perfect example! It deals with how God's sovereignty works when He is choosing to whom He shows mercy and compassion. "I *(God)* will show mercy to anyone I choose, and I will show compassion to anyone I choose" Romans 9:14 (NLT).

It is easy to pass by this Scripture without fully understanding because it is a very complicated concept for our finite minds. God's purpose is far beyond our understanding. The wonderful thing is that we who believe in Him have been chosen by Him to become part of His family and receive His mercy and compassion.

Here is an example from my finite mind. Say you went to an orphanage and wanted to adopt a child. They had 200 children who would meet your requirements, but one stood out to you. One you fell in love with just by looking at her. She, in turn wanted you as much as you did her. Therefore, you made your choice. Are you unfair because you did not choose the other 199? Not at all!

God chooses because He knows who will fulfill His purpose and because you bring Him pleasure. Of course, God's choice is much more complicated than this, but He chooses whomever He wants. Romans 9:17 says: "For the Scriptures say that God told Pharaoh,

I have appointed you for the very purpose of displaying my power in you and to spread my fame throughout the earth" (NLT). So you see, God chooses to show mercy to some, and He chooses to harden the hearts of others so they refuse to listen. It is complicated, but absolutely sovereign!

Personal Note:

While I was praying a few days ago, I received this picture in my mind. Millions of God's spirits awaiting their time to become human are together in heaven in a special place where God keeps them. With eyes of complete adoration, out of all of them, He reaches down and chooses me. He picks me up, places me lovingly in my mother's womb, and keeps me warm for nine months.

I was then born at exactly the moment in time that He had designed for me. Every detail of my life was meant to happen exactly as He planned it. Now that I was a human being, I also had to make a choice to receive His wonderful gift—His Son, Jesus Christ. When I did that, I became part of His heavenly family. My love for Him spilled over into tears of joy when He gave me this wonderful picture.

I am amazed every day, as I walk by faith in Him, how He continually blesses me and oh, how He cherishes me. Being cherished is something that I never felt until God so generously showed me how very much He loves me.

He loves you just as much—after all, He handpicked you at the exact moment in time to be His child as well! He lavishes all of us who are in His family with His matchless love and mercy and is preparing such a fabulous place for us to spend eternity with Him. It is beyond my understanding, but it is what brings my heavenly Father exuberant pleasure and joy.

Prayer:

Father, how I love You! I thank You so much for choosing me to be here on earth at this moment in time. I cannot begin to comprehend how full Your love is for me, but oh how grateful I am that I received

Jesus into my life and became Your child. I am overwhelmed by Your mercy and grace. Thank You! In Your Son's precious name, Jesus! Amen.

Your Reflections:

Day 36

God is . . . Generous

Bible Reading: Mark 10:13-16

When we think of the word "generous," we usually think of someone giving of his or her wealth to a person who is in real need. God certainly does that! Nevertheless, His generosity is different. He pours it out on all who come to Him with an open heart and empty hands. He gives freely to all who are seeking Him and come humbly before Him in childlike faith. It is simply our ability to give Him our all and turn our lives and problems over to Him. That is what brings about His generosity. The more we do this, the more He gives to us.

Jesus loved children! People brought their children to Him so that He would bless them. Some of His followers wanted to stop them; and Jesus said to them, "Let the little children come to me, don't stop them because the kingdom of God belongs to people just like that" Mark 10:14 (NCV). Little children are so wonderful! They are very trusting and pure so it is easy for them to believe almost anything that we tell them. God wants us to come to Him in this way.

In another Scripture, the disciples were with Him and they were discussing among themselves who was the greatest among them. Jesus asked them what they were talking about—they just remained silent because they did not want to admit the subject of their conversation. Jesus, of course, knew what they had been discussing; and He said, "Whoever wants to be the most important must be last of all and servant to all" Mark 9:29 (NLT). This was a hard concept for His followers and it is just as hard for us today.

As we grow up into adulthood, unfortunately, our childlike innocence disappears and we become skeptical, cynical and sometimes full of ourselves. Therefore, when God comes to us with such a simple plan for our redemption, it seems too easy. We think there must be strings attached or that we must have to help God out by being good. However, His generosity is exactly that simple. Matthew 5:3 reads, "Blessed are the poor in Spirit, for theirs is the kingdom of heaven" (NIV). When we realize that we are sinners and Jesus came to pay the price for our sin, and we come humbly before Him with a repentant heart, we then will receive the kingdom of God and all of His riches and glory. His generosity will be showered on us daily!

Personal Note:

This is one of the toughest things for me to remember as a Christian. Yes, I came with that childlike faith when I accepted Him into my life. Nevertheless, slowly, I tried to gain back my control in certain areas. My intent may have been to turn everything completely over to God; but there are certain things, even though my intent is good, my sinful nature may try to override and I have to yield to His control daily.

My heart wants to be His, 100%, but my human nature is always at war with God's best for me. Satan wants to control this area. It is only through moment-by-moment prayer that I can turn my selfish nature wholeheartedly over to Him. How wonderful it is to know that His generous grace and mercy are always right there to meet me at the point of my need. His grace is forever sufficient for me! How magnificent! What great love!

Prayer:

Father, I ask You to help me each day to be able to turn over all things to Your miraculous control. Thank You for being right there, to meet me exactly at my need. Every moment of every day, You help me to trust You as a little child trusts. In Jesus' Name, Amen.

Your Reflections:

Day 37

God is . . . Receptivity

Bible Reading: John 1:1-14

Receptivity is the very essence of life. When you plant a seed in the ground, it would lay there and die if it were not receptive to drinking in the water and the rich soil that is its cover. The only way that seed can bring forth productivity is to die to itself, receive the nutrients, and water that it is given. That is what God's kingdom is all about, receptivity.

God has always existed, but He wanted a being that He created who would be receptive to His purpose—one with whom He could commune. When man sinned, God still desired the same thing. He had a few loyal followers through the years that He could commune with, like Noah, Abraham, and Moses. There were more, of course, but as man grew and multiplied on the earth, they became less receptive to Him.

Through Moses, God gave His people the sacrifice of an animal as atonement for man's sin. At first the people were open to this plan, but as time passed, man became more and more evil and so God needed a permanent sacrificial lamb. His very own Son was willing to come to earth and die to be the provision that was needed in order to commune with God again. Why did God send His Son? There are more reasons, than we probably know, but the main purpose was His love for us. He wanted a human family that loved Him back and would commune with Him forever.

So now, through the blood of Jesus Christ, we can become a part of the family of God. We do that by receiving His blood sacrifice. "But to all who believe Him and accepted Him, He gave the right to become children of God. They are reborn—not with a physical birth resulting from human passion or plan, but a birth that comes from God" John 1:12-13 (NLT). What a simple plan He has for us . . . but sometimes how difficult it is for us to receive this wonderful gift. Yet God has the greatest blessing He could ever give us whenever we are receptive to His plan.

Personal Note:

Each day, as I walk with my Father, I pray for Him to open my heart to receive whatever He has for me that day. I wish I could say that I do everything I know He wants to do through me, but I am working toward that goal.

My heart longs to be receptive to His heart. Philippians 3:12-14 says it best. "I don't mean to say that I have already achieved these things or that I have already reached perfection, but I press on to possess that perfection for which Christ Jesus first possessed me. No, dear brothers and sisters, I have not achieved it but I focus on this one thing: forgetting the past and looking forward to what lies ahead, I press on to reach the end of the race and receive the heavenly prize for which God, through Christ Jesus is calling me." (NLT) Every day that I reach toward the goal of receiving His best for me, I am getting closer to that objective. It is a learning process filled with blessing that I cannot even articulate. How rewarding! How like God!

Prayer:

Thank You, Father, that each day is more blessed than the day before. You fulfill my every desire when I am living in Your purpose. I praise You because You reached down and chose me to be in Your family. The blessings never stop flowing! How I love You and thank You, in Jesus' Name, Amen.

Your Reflections:

Day 38

God is . . . Contentment

Bible Reading: Philippians 4:4-12

Contentment is something that many of us lack in our lives today. It seems that discontent is all around us. We live in a society that keeps wanting more and more. The electronic age is moving so fast that if you have a two-year-old computer or other equipment, you are very outdated. That is if you are trying to keep up with the current capabilities.

Cell phones are continually updated so we can now send text messages, e-messages, surf the internet and many other things as well. Many, instead of talking to each other face to face, spend hours on just text messaging back and forth!

You barely know what the latest style is before it changes again. Our kitchen, which we remodeled in 2002, was outdated by the time we finished remodeling it. Nevertheless, amid all of the madness surrounding us, there is one constant. Our Father, who is our stable contentment. "But Jesus Christ is the same, yesterday, today and forever!" Hebrews 13:8 (NIV). He is the only "constant" in a turbulent world.

Paul knew the secret of being content. In Philippians 4:11-13 he wrote, "I am not saying this because I am in need, for I have learned to be content whatever the circumstances. I know what it is to be in need, and I know what it is to have plenty. I have learned the secret of being content in any and every situation, whether well fed or hungry, whether living in plenty or in want. I can do everything through

Him who gives me strength" (NIV). What an amazing statement! Paul, who suffered so often, was beaten, had to flee for his life, was in and out of prison and was scorned and scoffed at—yet he knew the secret of being content—doing everything through Christ! Jesus is our contentment as well!

Personal Note:

I am learning that the more often I can turn over all of my life concerns to my Father, the more content I become. He does not want me to go around carrying a heavy load of cares and stresses. He is my contentment. He fulfills my every need. Oh, I forget sometimes, but in time, I come back to the peace and contentment that only He can bring.

In fact, I think that many lessons can be wrapped up in this one word, contentment. I cannot think of any one word that I need more often in my life on a daily basis. When there is not enough "day" to go around, when I am hit head on with a serious problem, when a loved one dies, when a person fails me; worse still when I fail someone else who is depending on me, what is the one thing that stabilizes my day? Christ is the answer to true contentment. Yes, I too, can do everything through Him who gives me strength day in and day out! What wonderful grace He bestows on me—all I have to do is ask Him for it!

Prayer:

Father, You are contentment. You are all I need to solve every situation that arises. Help me to draw on Your strength, which is available to me just for the asking. You are my source of peace, my secure place. I thank You so much! In Jesus' Name, Amen.

Your Reflections:

Day 39

God is . . . A Masterful Touch

Bible Reading: Luke 8:40-48

When Jesus was here on earth, one of His most constant ministries was healing the sick and raising people from the dead. There are many accounts in the gospels of His miraculous acts. Today's reading overflows with the power and touch of our Master. In all of the accounts of His numerous healings the one that stands out most to me, was done very innocently and privately.

It is the account where Jesus was on His way to heal Jairus' daughter. The crowd was so thick and packed that they could hardly move. All of a sudden, Jesus stopped and said, "Who touched me?" What an odd question when the multitude was pressed tightly around Him. His disciples were quick to call His attention to that fact saying, "'What do you mean who touched you?" Jesus said; 'No, this was different! Power went out of my body by someone who was not afraid to believe for a miracle.'"

He stopped; and His eyes scanned the crowd. Then they rested on a specific woman. Verses 47-48 tells us, "Then the woman, seeing that she could not go unnoticed, came trembling and fell at His feet; in the presence of all the people, she told Him why she had touched Him and how she had been instantly healed" (NIV). You see, she had been struggling with a bleeding disorder for twelve years; and no doctor had been able to help her. Nevertheless, one simple faltering touch of the hem of Christ's garment and she was made entirely whole.

The difference was that she purposely sought out Jesus because she believed that if she could touch even His clothing, she would be healed. In verse 48, we read, "'Then He said to her, 'Daughter, your faith has healed you. Go in peace'" (NIV). He is just as touchable today! He wants us to reach out to Him and just touch His garment. That is all the faith it takes. When we do, His power will be released in us and He will take us places that we never dreamed!

Personal Note:

Just a touch from the Master—that is all I need! When I reach out my arms toward Him, He will always meet me more than halfway. Every day, as I start my day with Him, I reach out for the Master's touch to take me through the day. He forever joins me, exactly where my need is! He gives me strength and power to sustain me today. That is all I need . . . just a masterful touch from Him today. Tomorrow, He will be there just waiting for me to reach out to Him again. I can hardly wait for tomorrow!

Prayer:

Father, how intimately You care for me! You are so touchable—so available. Help me to grow in faith, so that I can always reach out and know that You are there just waiting for me to draw on Your power and love. I yearn for another touch from You. In Your powerful name, Jesus! Amen.

Your Reflections:

Day 40

God is . . . Lingering

Bible Reading: Luke 19:1-10

How do we get God's attention? One of the most effective ways is by recognizing that we need and desire Him. When Jesus was here on earth, you would find Him with the poor, the rejected, and the needy people, the ones that society would call outcasts.

Zacchaeus was such a man. He was one of those horrible rich tax collectors who were hated by everyone. He knew that Jesus was going to pass by, and He yearned to glimpse Him. He was a short man in stature, so he could not see above the crowds. There was absolutely no way that anyone in the throng was going to move over and help him. He wanted to see Jesus so much that he decided to climb a tree so that he could at least watch Him as He passed by.

As Zacchaeus observed Jesus from his perch in the sycamore tree, he had a clear view. Nevertheless, something was happening! Jesus was lingering right below him. Then Jesus raised His eyes, looked right at him, and said, "Zacchaeus hurry and come down! I must stay at your house today" Luke 19:5 (NCV). My, how that caused a stir in the crowd. People were murmuring that Jesus was going to reside with a sinner! How could He be the Son of God and socialize with such a vile man! In verse 10 Jesus replied to the crowd, "The Son of Man came to find lost people and save them." (NCV). This event totally changed the life and direction of Zacchaeus. It will change your direction as well!

Personal Note:

This has always been one of my favorite stories recorded in the gospels. I guess one reason is that I am short and can relate with not being able to see when I am in a crowd. I more than likely would have climbed a tree as well. I do not even go places where a crowd is lined up unless it is very special, because I know it is useless for me to try to see anything.

The second reason that I like this story is because even before Zacchaeus realized that he had a valid need in his life, Jesus was already there just lingering around, waiting for Zacchaeus to become aware of his desire. That is what He does in my life as well. Before I realize that I have a need, Jesus is already there. Just staying close by, waiting for me to realize that I long for Him! When I am "up a tree," He is looking up at me and saying, "Clarice, come down, I must spend time with you today!" I love the word "must" in this translation. Not only does Jesus want to spend time with me, there is urgency in His voice. I must spend time with you today!

He is waiting, lingering close, to say those very words to you too! Can you feel Him lingering, waiting? He will totally change your life! What an awesome concept! How thankful I am that He has an urgency to meet my deepest need. Oh that I might keep a seeking heart so that I am ready whenever He comes calling on me!

Prayer:

Father, thank You that You are ever lingering close, just waiting for me to invite you into a deeper place in my heart and life. Help me to keep my heart open and pure before You, so that You may come and dine with me anytime! In Jesus' name, Amen.

Your Reflections:

Day 41

God is . . . Our Mysterious Planner

Bible Reading: Ephesians 3: 7-12

Throughout the Old Testament, it was very clear who God's chosen ones were. His plan was for Israel to be His people and then He would be their God. As revealed in the four gospels, when Jesus came to earth, people did not even think of anyone else other than a Jew being a part of God's family.

Jesus showed them on several occasions how He blessed a hated Gentile. One of the best examples of this was the woman of Samaria. Samaritans were particularly hated by the Jews. In fact, a Jew would take a longer route just to bypass Samaria because they hated them so much. Actually, Jesus gave two examples in the gospels just to let the Jews know that His love reached everyone. They did not "get the point" though. It was not until Jesus rose from the grave and had ascended into heaven that the apostles began to understand that God had a different plan now.

Even then, in their minds they were to witness only to the Jewish people. The disciple Philip was really the first to go as a missionary to the Gentiles. He witnessed to an Ethiopian eunuch without any restraint. Nevertheless, the one who finally accepted God's calling and to whom God revealed His greater plan was Paul. In Ephesians 3: 5-6 he writes, "God did not reveal it to previous generations, but now by His Spirit He has revealed it to His holy apostles and prophets. And this is God's plan: both Gentiles and Jews who believe the Good News share equally in the riches inherited by God's children. Both are part of the same body, and both enjoy the promise of blessings because they belong to Christ Jesus" (NLT). How awesome! Now God showed them there is no prejudice in His kingdom. No one is excluded from God's eternal family! No more mystery, just extreme love and grace!

Personal Note:

We take for granted so much today! I wonder how many of us really realize as we sit in our comfortable pews, in "Christian" churches, that we owe our whole salvation to the Jews. Do we remember that Christ was Jewish? Paul and all of the Apostles were also Jewish. I really did not think a lot about that. I was raised to love the Jewish people, but until recently, it was not something for which I gave much consideration. Unfortunately, many of us feel that way.

The events that are taking place in Israel today affect us as Christians. We need to uphold our Jewish friends in prayer because we are family with Israel! The Jews were missionaries to us first. God in His mercy and grace included us to be a part of this mighty family! How very grateful I am that He did!

Prayer:

Father, as I realize how You revealed Your plan to us through the Apostles in the birthing of Your church, how grateful I am that You included me in that plan. Help me to love my Christian and Jewish brothers and sisters alike, because we are all a part of Your mysterious plan. In Jesus' precious name, Amen.

Your Reflections:

Day 42

God is . . . A Comforting Helper

Bible Reading: John 16:7-15

Before Jesus was crucified, He had many conversations with His disciples, but this particular one was very disturbing to them. Jesus was telling them that He was going away! They had great difficulty in comprehending what he was telling them. He was talking about leaving them and going back to the One who sent Him. Christ knew they could not understand what He was saying, but He also knew they would be able to assimilate all of this later.

He was comforting them by telling them that He must leave, but that when He did He would send the Helper to be with them. The New Century Version reads, "When the Helper comes, He will prove to the people of the world the truth about sin, about being right with God and about judgment." John 16:8

Who is the Helper that Jesus would send? It is the Holy Spirit. Depending on your translation, in this passage the Holy Spirit is called the Comforter, the Advocate and the Helper and further down in the passage the Spirit of Truth. The Holy Spirit's main "job description" is all wrapped up in that one verse. He will convict of sin, show us how to live righteously and tell us about God's judgment. The Holy Spirit leads us into all knowledge of Christ.

"But when the Spirit of Truth comes, He will guide you into all truth. He will not speak His own words, but He will speak only what He hears. The Spirit of Truth will bring glory to Me because He will take what I have to say and tell it to you" John 16:13-14 (NLT). How awesome is that! The Spirit will speak directly to us from Christ's own lips! I want to listen very carefully, so that I do not miss one word of truth! What a fabulous God we serve!

Personal Note:

As I consider yet another aspect of this amazing God, how sobering it is for me to think of all of the conversations the Holy Spirit might have had about me and I was too busy to listen. You see, not only does He bring the words that Christ wants me to hear; He also takes the words that I am saying back to Jesus, who then speaks on my behalf to the Father.

As I dig deeper into the heart of the triune God, it makes me much more aware of the intimacy that the Father wants to have with me. It also makes me more attentive to the words I speak. I want my words to reflect His glory. I certainly am not there yet, but my heart's desire is to reflect Jesus through every part of my life. We sang a song quite often when I was growing up. It was titled, "Let the Beauty of Jesus Be Seen in Me." That is my objective.

Prayer:

Father, thank You for teaching me another of Your truths. Help me to guard my words and allow Your Spirit to grow in me and fill me to overflowing with Your love and grace. In Jesus' name, Amen.

Your Reflections:

Day 43

God is . . . A Faithful Consolation

Bible Reading: Isaiah 61:1-8

It seems that our lives are filled with many mountains and valleys. As we follow the history of Israel, we certainly see this when it comes to their trust in God. In fact, God constantly had to console and then judge His people. He would bring someone into their lives that would bring them great victory, and they would turn to God and worship Him. But it only took a few years before they would go back to worshipping other gods, forgetting the true and living God.

This was the atmosphere of the children of Israel during the time of all of the prophets. The people would turn away and then they would have to go through horrible trials. Many times, they were even exiled and enslaved before they would repent. God would bring them back again, console them and start showering them with His favor once more.

A day is coming, however, when Israel will be the apple of God's eye once more. In our Scripture today, Isaiah wrote in verse 7, "Instead of their shame my people will receive a double portion, and instead of disgrace, they will rejoice in their inheritance; and so they will inherit a double portion in their land and everlasting joy will be theirs" (NIV).

He does the same for us today. As heirs with Him, when we are obedient to His plan for us, no matter how many trials we go through, He will always be there to comfort us. He brings us the encouragement we need to continue to be faithful to Him.

2 Thessalonians 2:16-17 says, "May our Lord Jesus Christ Himself and God our Father, who loved us and by His grace gave us eternal encouragement and good hope, encourage your hearts and strengthen you in every good deed and word" (NIV). He never promised us an easy road, but He has promised to encourage us along the way when we are obedient to Him. Now that is real consolation!

Personal Note:

I have been through many rough spots during my life, as we all have. Nevertheless, when I am almost consumed by the darkness, I look up and there is His light shining brightly at the end of the tunnel. Sometimes, the tunnel is extensive and bumpy, but as long as I have my eyes focused on the light, I know that He will be there at the end to console, encourage and bring me gladness and a joyful heart.

He has never failed to bless me when the trial is over, and He never will! The more difficulties that I experience, the more blessing He will pour over me and build me up to bless others, because I can now relate to what they are facing. Moreover, it has always been worth the sorrow, shame, or hurt. What joy and consolation that brings!

Prayer:

Father, I know that Your ways are not my ways; but I thank You that even when I must go through deep waters, You are always there to rescue me and to comfort me. How I praise You for that! In Jesus' name, Amen.

Your Reflections:

Day 44

God is . . . My Grief Bearer

Bible Reading: Isaiah 53:1-7

This is one of the most beautiful and yet heart-wrenching passages of the Bible—at least it is for me. Isaiah paints a sobering picture of Christ's suffering. It is interesting that one of the first things that happened to Jesus in this passage of Scripture is when Isaiah talks about our Lord's suffering. "He was despised and rejected by men, a man of sorrows, and familiar with suffering" Isaiah 53:3 (NIV).

In every account of His death, the Bible talks about how He suffered and felt sorrow and grief. Before Christ was nailed to the cross, He already had endured so much. He felt rejected, betrayed by His friends, despised by His chosen people, spit at, ridiculed, tortured and beaten almost to death, yet He did not complain or utter a word. He bore everything that we would ever feel or need before He went to the cross.

The cross was the ultimate climax of cleansing us from our sin, so that His atonement would be the decisive conclusion of all He had already completed for us. There is no one in history who has ever suffered more than our Lord has. His suffering would atone for the worst of what we would suffer, so that He literally carried the burden of everything we would go through in our lives. He did it entirely because of His deep love for us!

God has always cared about our suffering and grief. He wants us to come to Him so that He can help us through these very deep trials when they arise. If we allow Him to carry our grief, our burden will be much lighter than those who do not know Him as their Savior. "For He has rescued us from the dominion of darkness and brought us into the kingdom of the Son He loves, in whom we have redemption, the forgiveness of sins" Colossians 1:13-14 (NIV). His love transcends anything we could ever think or feel! How sublime!

Personal Note:

Sometimes sorrow and grief can turn out to be a blessing, when we are open to God's protection. I remember when my two sisters were killed in an auto accident and we had a double funeral. Some people criticized me because they thought that I was "doing too well"—that I did not care. The truth was that God knew that I had to be the strength for my mother and other sister. He wrapped His arms around me and I felt His presence so vividly that I became the "rock" that my family needed.

During that trying time, God gave me a song that has been with me through every situation for more than 40 years. "His Eye is On the Sparrow." The lyric of the first verse reads:

> *"Why should I feel discouraged, why should the shadows fall,*
> *Why should my heart feel lonely and long for heaven and home.?*
> *When Jesus is my portion, a constant friend is He,*
> *For His eye is on the sparrow and I know He watches me.*
> *His eye is on the sparrow, and I know He watches me.*
> *CHORUS:*
> *I sing because I'm happy, I sing because I'm free!*
> *For His eye is on the sparrow . . . and I know He watches me."*

To this day, when I am under extreme stress, I find myself singing that song in my head. My Grief Bearer has never let me down in all these years, and He never will.

Prayer:

Father, thank You that You know and feel every sorrow and grief that I go through. Thank You for Your strength in times of need and for the song that You placed in my heart. In Jesus' name, Amen.

Your Reflections:

Day 45

God is . . . Kindhearted

Bible Reading: Isaiah 63:7-10

Sometimes it is very easy to take God's kindness to us for granted. Just like all the other blessings in our life, good health, having a roof over our heads, or transportation to wherever we need to go, we are no different from the Israelites of old. We just assume that these things are automatically ours.

God showed His kindness to His people repeatedly. Nevertheless, each time they seemed to forget and take Him for granted. Isaiah 63:7 reads, "I will mention the loving-kindnesses of the Lord and the praises of the Lord, according to all that the Lord has bestowed on us, and the great goodness toward the house of Israel, which He has bestowed on them according to His mercies, according to the multitude of His loving kindnesses" (NKJ).

I love how the New King James version uses the words "multitude of His loving kindnesses." A multitude to me means so many that we cannot even count. That is what He does for us, as well. His blessings (another word for favor or kindness) are beyond counting. Sometimes when I am reading the Word, especially the Old Testament, I look at Israel and what God has done for them and think, I would not turn my back on God if I saw all of the miracles that they saw! However, when I look at my own struggles I realize that none of us ever knows what we are capable of in any given circumstance.

I am learning to judge others less, because judging is a form of arrogance. As a human being, I am capable of anything and that is one of the reasons that Christ told us not to judge.

Nehemiah wrote, "They refused to obey, and they were not mindful of Your wonders that You did among them. But they hardened their necks, and in their rebellion, they appointed a leader to return to their bondage. But You are God, ready to pardon, gracious and merciful, slow to anger, abundant in kindness and did not forsake them" Nehemiah 9:17 (NKJ). How mindful of God's wonders are we? I am on a personal journey to remember His kindness and to become mindful of everything about the magnificent God that I serve. How thankful I am that I serve a God of mercy and kindness. How it fills my heart with joy!

Personal Note:

Taking God's kindness for granted . . . . WOW! I have to admit, I have done that too many times. As I continually grow in Him and He points out all of these areas that I did not really think about—is so humbling. I try to open my prayer time with Him each day, with praises of Him and blessings that He has bestowed on me. Often, my mind will not recall a new blessing at first. It is only after my real praise time, that I can start counting my blessings, but I know that I do not even scratch the surface of what He has done in my life. I pray that I will become more attentive to His kindnesses toward me.

Prayer:

Oh Father, I fall so short of Your mark. I thank You for Your mercy and loving-kindness and that You never give up on me. You are gracious and forgiving. How thankful I am that You will never leave me or forsake me. Thank You for Your blessings in my life. In Jesus' name, Amen.

Your Reflections:

Day 46

God is . . . A Thought Changer

Bible Reading: Psalm 139:1-6

In a world that is growing ever more public and our lives less private, one thing is for certain, we still have thoughts that no one else will ever know. That can be a great comfort if our thoughts are unkind or shameful. If we have a judgmental thought about someone, it is good that they cannot read our minds. Nevertheless, the other side of the coin is, how many times have I thought something good and encouraging about someone but did not say anything? Perhaps I could have changed a bad day into a good one for somebody.

There is no doubt about it, thoughts are still something that we can keep to ourselves and nobody need know that we even had them. There is One, however, who knows every thought that we ever had or ever will have. He knows what we are going to say even before we say it. In our reading today we read, "Before a word is on my tongue You know it completely, O Lord" Psalm 139:4 (NIV). Yes, the God who created us knows our every thought. There is nowhere that we can go where God will not know us and know our thoughts.

The awesome thing is, though, that He loves us anyway and in everyway. We play so many games with each other and put on a facade to make ourselves "nicer people" to each other, but God already knows what we are like inside and still cherishes us! "Such knowledge is too wonderful for me, too lofty for me to attain" Psalm 139:6 (NIV). He is the one person with whom we can be entirely real. It is a great comfort to me that I can come to Him with everything.

He already knows all about it and is waiting for me to express it! How very precious and powerful that is!

Personal Note:

One of the things that have often been difficult for me is concentration. My thoughts can just wander all over the place. This is another area where I have been asking for my Father's help! Sometimes when I pray, my thoughts are completely scattered. I want them to be focused on Him. He has encouraged me tremendously just in the past few months.

In fact, recently I was able to effectively focus on His love for me in a deeper way. No talking, no thoughts straying away, just pure worship to the One who has changed my life so dramatically. I worshipped Him in this way for quite a while. If my mind began drifting I would look up and say, Father, help me to focus back on You, and He did! I realized how much He has helped bring my thoughts under His control. Consequently, I am much calmer and more peaceful now than I have ever been before. "Oh, how I praise You Father; I am so awed by You!"

Prayer:

Thank You my Father, for being my thought changer. You alone know every thought and intent of my heart. I rejoice because I am fearfully and wonderfully made, and You love me so dearly. How I praise You and cherish every thought that I have of You. In Jesus' mighty name, Amen.

Your Reflections:

Day 47

God is . . . My Heart Holder

Bible Reading: Psalm 18:28-36

When we are in sorrow over a hurt or a wrong done to us, it is an agonizing feeling. We feel like we have reached rock bottom and it is a very vulnerable time. It is easy to listen to the negative messages that go on in our heads just below the level of utterance—in our thought processes. Sometimes, as we wallow in self pity, we may even tell ourselves that whatever hurt we are feeling we of course deserve, because we are not worthy of anything better.

That is a lie straight from Satan himself! We are children of the King of kings and Lord of lords! We are beautifully and wonderfully made. God has never made anything inferior and He never will. We are fashioned after His very image, reaching in the direction of becoming more and more like Him. We are the apple of His eye, and He holds our hearts lovingly next to His heart.

When we are hurting deeply our Father wants us to turn to Him for comfort. David wrote, "It is God who arms me with strength and makes my way perfect" Psalm 18:32 (NIV). My God is a God of the positive. He alone can give me the strength I need when the waters get too deep, and I feel like I am going to drown in the mire of my stress and pressure.

When my heart is breaking, that is when I need to look up to the One who has been through it all. Isaiah 53:3 says, "He was despised and rejected by men, a man of sorrows and familiar with suffering.

Like one from whom men hide their faces He was despised, and we esteemed Him not" (NIV).

Jesus is just waiting to hold our hearts next to His and say, "I understand, my child! I have paid the price of your suffering. You do not need to carry it any longer. Let Me carry your load. I love you more than you will ever know. Your burdens are so important to Me! Give them to Me! Let Me carry them for you. Rest in Me and I will give you My peace and comfort!" Jesus said, "Peace I leave with you; My peace I give you, I do not give to you as the world gives. Do not let your heart be troubled and do not be afraid" John 14:27 (NIV). Only Christ can hold your heart next to His and give you that kind of comfort.

Personal Note:

God's ways are so amazing. Before I knew that this was the subject for today, I was feeling down and discouraged and I shared some concerns with someone I care deeply about, who, of course, was going through her own dark time. In my email, I hurt her because she was so very vulnerable. If I had not been "wallowing a bit," I would have known that what I said would hurt her. Even though I only allowed myself a short time to feel self-pity, it was long enough to hurt someone that is very dear to me. Words, whether they are spoken or written, can never be taken back. My intention was good but had I talked to my heavenly Father about this before I talked to her, I would not have sent that email.

I can cause someone else pain and sorrow so quickly if I do not think, but just barge ahead. Whether it is a spouse, a friend or a relative, love is never the issue. My own self-pity, self-centeredness and selfish desires are what create most of the hurts I inflict on others.

Of course, we were both very sorry, but had I just prayed first, how much grief I could have spared both of us. 2 Corinthians 1:3-4 says: "Praise be to the God and Father of our Lord Jesus Christ, the Father of compassion and the God of all comforts, who comforts us in all our troubles, so that we can comfort those in any trouble with the comfort we ourselves have received from God" (NIV). I hope that I can say, "Lesson learned!"

Prayer:

Father, how thankful I am that You are a God of forgiveness. That when I come to You with my concerns and hurts that You hold my heart close to Yours and bring me rest for my soul. Help me to call upon You first, because I know You are the God of all comfort and You will embrace me and comfort me. Help me to remember that You are my burden-lifter. In Jesus' name, Amen.

Your Reflections:

Day 48

God is . . . Abiding

Bible Reading: Colossians 2:2-10

"Abiding" is a word that we do not use often today. What is abiding? It is not even in the 75,000 entries in my Webster's Dictionary. It is used in the newer translations with words such as continuing, remaining, and dwelling. God does all of those in our lives. In verse 6 of today's reading it reads, "So then, just as you received Christ Jesus as Lord, continue to live in Him, rooted and built up in Him, strengthened in the faith as you were taught, and overflowing with thankfulness" (NIV). So many Christians today do not even know how to abide. It is a deep grounding in Him achieved only through our total submission to Him.

We spend more time "striving" than "abiding." We keep trying to live the Christian life, trying to have faith, and trying to turn our cares over to Him. We keep failing, and then we have a guilt trip and we ask His forgiveness. We start a new day, and try again to live the kind of life we know we should live, but we fall short again—more guilt. Some of us live our entire lives without ever realizing that we did not need to strive to DO anything!

All God really wants of us is to quit striving (being stressed out) and just abide in Him! When we learn to abide or remain in Him, all of a sudden our struggles are no longer there. We are now learning to let Him endure for us. John 15:7 says, If you remain in Me and My words remain in you, ask whatever you wish, and it will be given you" (NIV). What a fabulous promise!

It is such an easy solution to our problems; I do not know why it is so hard to do. For most of us though, we just keep stressing out. We like to control things and abiding requires letting go of our problem and placing it in His control. John 15:10 reads "If you keep My commandments, you will abide in My love, just as I have kept My Father's commandments and abide in His love" (NKJ). I want to learn to abide in Him in everything. I know that my Lord will be there just waiting for me to abide in His fullness.

Personal Note:

I am learning to abide in Him. When I fail, I am much quicker to come to Him because when I am striving, it is just not fun! It is hard and wearing on my body, soul and spirit. I am depressed and feel blue and empty. I am not a quick learner, so it has taken me a lifetime to be able to abide in Him even a good portion of the time. When I do, Colossians 3:15 becomes my life. It reads, "Let the peace of Christ rule in your hearts, since as members of one body you were called to peace, and always be thankful" (NIV). I was called to abide! When I am worried or stressed, it is hard to be at peace and be thankful. He has called me to live in peace. Only through abiding in Him can I do so. He has so much fullness and joy just waiting for me as I allow my spirit to rest in Him.

Prayer:

Father, You have promised so much peace and thanksgiving. Help me to submit to You and learn to abide in You, as You abide in me. There is so much calmness and rest awaiting me as I learn, day by day, to abide in You. Help me to grow deeply in You as I am strengthened by You. In Jesus' name, Amen.

Your Reflections:

Day 49

God is . . . A Steadying Spirit

Bible Reading: 2 Corinthians 1:18-23

Paul is probably the most effective preacher and teacher to us as Gentiles. At least we have many more writings by him than we do the other Apostles. God used him in a mighty way in the early church. He teaches us through His struggles and confidences in our Lord and Savior. He introduces us to the way that God is now going to work in and through us. God's Holy Spirit dwells within all of us who receive Jesus Christ as our personal Savior, both Jew and Gentile. That is only the beginning of what God can, and will, work through our lives as believers.

As we learn to trust Him more, He gives us a confidence within, which brings us great stability and keeps us steady in our walk with Him. Verse 21 reads, "Now it is God who makes both us and you stand firm in Christ. He anointed us, set His seal of ownership on us, and put His Spirit in our hearts as a deposit, guaranteeing what is to come" (NIV). What a powerful verse! We never need to waiver in our faith and hope when we put our trust in Him. He is the steadying force that helps us get through the hard spots in life.

We are called to boldly walk in a way that will further His work. 2 Corinthians 2:14-15 is a wonderful Scripture that has greatly blessed me. "But thanks be to God, who always leads us in triumphal procession in Christ and through us spreads everywhere the fragrance of the knowledge of Him. For we are to God the aroma of Christ among those who are being saved and those who are perishing" (NIV). What a magnificent verse! I want to spread forth the aroma of Christ, so everyone will know that I have the very fragrance of life living in and through me. What a wonderful picture! How blessed I am to be a part of this wonderful Kingdom!

Personal Note:

I don't know why the Lord is leading me to give you such a personal glimpse into my life and my struggles. It makes me feel very vulnerable. However, I can count on God's strength perfecting me through this process.

Paul had to face up to many personal things in his life as well. In fact, God gave him a "thorn in the flesh" to keep him humble and trusting Him. I, too, rely on the verse that Paul wrote in 2 Corinthians 12:9, 10, "But He said to me, My grace is sufficient for you, for my power is made perfect in weakness. Therefore I will boast all the more gladly about my weaknesses, so that Christ's power may rest on me" (NIV).

I know that a year ago, I could not have written this devotional. It would have been abhorrent to me to expose my weaknesses. Now, however, I just let my Father take me where He guides my heart and fingers and type away. I desire to have that steadying Spirit at work constantly in my life.

If it means that I must expose my flaws, then as Paul so aptly wrote, "That is why for Christ's sake, I delight in weaknesses . . . for when I am weak, then I am strong!" 2 Corinthians 12:10 (NIV) (excerpts). He has me on a rock solid foundation, so that when turmoil comes upon me, I know, without a doubt that He will sustain me, and make me stronger. Each time I fail, I come back to Him sooner and in humble adoration look to the steadying spirit of my Lord and Savior. I know that I have sure footing as I walk with Him.

Prayer:

Father, keep me firm and secure as I walk one step at a time with You. Thank You for the steadying Spirit that You have given me. I know that I can always rely on You! Thank You, In Jesus' name, Amen.

Your Reflections:

Day 50

God is . . . Meek

Bible Reading: Matthew 5:1-5

Meekness is a quality that has been vastly misunderstood. If you asked many Americans what that word means they would say, "It means someone who lets you walk all over them!" Nothing could be further from the truth. The newer translations of the Bible usually use the word humble rather than meek. Humbleness plays a part in meekness, but it does not encompass this spiritual quality.

Christ was meek. He certainly was not a milquetoast wimpy personality. He was not passive in any way. He certainly did not let people run all over Him. He was extremely kindhearted, gentle, compassionate, peaceful, patient and humble. All of these qualities and many more are all enveloped in the one quality of meekness. In Matthew 11:28, 29, Christ lets us know that meekness is a quality to be desired. It reads, "Come to Me, all of you who are weary and carry heavy burdens and I will give you rest. Take my yoke upon you. Let Me teach you, because I am humble and gentle at heart and you will find rest for your souls. For My yoke is easy to bear, and the burden I give you is light" (NLT). In verse 29, the King James Version reads, "Take my yoke upon you, and learn of Me; for I am meek and lowly in heart and ye shall find rest unto your souls."

Desiring to become meek, is a fabulous spiritual objective. Meekness is where we find rest for our souls. Jesus said in our reading today verse 5, "Blessed are the meek, for they shall inherit the earth." (NKJ). It takes great strength to be a caretaker of the earth. It takes a great quality for God to want to turn over the whole earth to us. I don't know how you feel, but I would be overwhelmed inheriting a castle. I can't even imagine what it will be like to inherit the earth! However, I want to find out. This is definitely a quality that I cherish!

Personal Note:

It would please me if someone describing me said that I had the quality of meekness. I love the fact that we cannot really define it in human terms. It is one of the things that make meekness so wonderful to achieve. It is the quality that Jesus defined Himself as having. It is a place of gentleness and peace. A place where I can relax through the situation not be uptight and worried. It is a place of confident rest in Him.

Humility and gentleness both sound so restful and serene to me. What a wonderful life it would be if I could attain meekness, so that inside of me there would be this protective bubble of strength, so that none of Satan's fiery darts could penetrate it, and none of my human insecurities could ever touch it. It is a place that I will attain when I get to heaven. For now, though, I reach toward that mark of the high calling of meekness!

Prayer:

Oh, Father, How precious You are to me. How I long to attain the goal of meekness. I thank You that You are teaching me day by day so many things that I want to reach toward and attain. Thank you for each step that You have brought me on this fabulous journey. In Jesus' powerful name, Amen.

Your Reflections:

Day 51

God is . . . Solid Assurance

Bible Reading: 2 Corinthians 4:7-10, 16-18

Paul had a real transformation in his life when he encountered our Lord Jesus Christ on the road to Damascus. His life exuded confidence and assurance. How could it not, when he literally saw Jesus sitting at the right hand of God the Father in heaven? During his ministry, he also was transported into the third heaven and saw things that he could not begin to describe. Because of this, God gave him something in his life to keep him humble. He called it a "thorn in the flesh." Yet with all of that, he remained solid in his faith and did not take his salvation for granted.

This is one of the reasons why he was able to write with such certainty. He knew that without Christ, he could do nothing. He had the quality of meekness. 2 Corinthians 10:1, 2 reads, "Now I, Paul, appeal to you with the gentleness and kindheartedness of Christ—though I realize you think I am timid in person and bold only when I write from far away. Well, I am begging you now, so that when I come I won't have to be bold with those who think we act from human motives" (NLT).

He had no problem at all trusting the One who so miraculously saved him. Paul continues, "It is written: I believe; therefore I have spoken. With that same spirit of faith we also believe and therefore speak" 2 Corinthians 4:13 (NIV). He had a solid assurance that everything was under Christ's sovereign control, and there really was no question about it! Firm, solid, that was Paul's faith!

Personal Note:

As far as salvation is concerned, "it is written therefore I believe it!" Nothing more needs to be said. However, is my faith as I walk with Christ as solid as I want it to be? When I am abiding in Him, I have that strong assurance, but there are moments when I still waiver in some areas. Do I truly trust Him as Paul did? Oh, in my heart I desire to! However, in reality and living day by day consistently abiding in His grace, there are moments when I doubt. I praise Him for the growth that I have experienced thus far, but I yearn for the time that my heart and humanness can be united with Him, in all things.

I know that none of us achieves perfection, but I am humbled by the journey I am traveling with Him. I pray that each day, my faith will continue to grow stronger and my stubborn will can be brought increasingly under His control. Hebrews 10:22a reads, "Let us draw near to God with a sincere heart in full assurance of faith" (NIV). He is my solid assurance.

Prayer:

Father, You are the rock on which I stand. You are my strength and my salvation. How I praise You as You continually work to make me into the uniqueness that You have for only me. Help me to keep abiding in You. In Jesus' name, Amen.

Your Reflections:

Day 52

God is . . . Ageless Consistency

Bible Reading: Hebrews 10:21-25

For some Christians, it is hard to believe that Jesus Christ is the same yesterday, today and forever. We say we believe, nonetheless, if we truly believed we would have no problems with knowing that God is in every move that we make.

His sovereign purpose would be performed in us, even in times when we cannot see His plan or when we are in a deep and hurtful situation. We would believe that every ailment in our body can literally be healed and that nothing happens by circumstance. Everything, even the smallest detail, is under the permissive will of God because He alone knows the complete long-term purpose for everything.

Since He dramatically healed me, from a life in a wheelchair and healed my surgery worn knee so that I could walk again, I take a lot more things literally, than I used to. However, I do not always have a spectacular miracle happen. Then it really comes down to do I believe that He works today just as He did in Abraham's day, or David's or Paul's? The Bible is meaningless if I cannot trust it. Hebrews 10:23 reads, "Let us hold firmly to the hope that we have confessed, because we can trust God to do what He promised" (NCT). It is truly all about hope and trust. He has proven that He is faithful to me, so I can trust His ageless consistency!

Personal Note:

One of the hard things for me to deal with is that I am an excellent "forgetter." That is, it is easy for me to forget what happened in the past. We are not to dwell on the past, but it is good for us to remember the many times that God worked on our behalf. That is why I now write down dates and celebrate the events when He worked a special thing in my life. For instance on October 19, 1998, I had a mastectomy and still no sign of cancer returning. On June 14, 2005, He miraculously healed my crippled knee. I could not walk, now I walk freely! March 8, 2006, He persuaded me to start writing this devotional; and He is taking me places that I have never dreamed about before.

I believe the Jewish people have more religious holidays or feast days than any other people. They are sacred, because God performed great miracles for them. God instructed them to remember each one by a celebration every year. He performs the same for us today.

I was led to start celebrating these particular days, because He has changed my life dramatically on each one of them. I wish that I could go back further, and maybe He will bring specific dates to mind, but for now, these three will be celebrated each year as a remembrance of His ageless consistency in performing great things in my life. I look forward to meeting all the other saints and rejoicing with them in what He did for me, even as He did for them. What a marvelous day that will be! Best of all, I will be able to thank Christ in person for all of the mighty deeds He did in my life!

Prayer:

Father, how thankful I am that You never change. That You perform great and powerful deeds today just as You did in the past. Help me to trust You more each day as I walk in Your love and grace. In Jesus' name, Amen.

Your Reflections:

Day 53

God is . . . A Fatherly Corrector

Bible Reading: Numbers 12:1-8

When the children of Israel were traveling through the wilderness, God was always present with them. However, to Moses, He was like a loving Father. God watched out for Moses, even when his own brother and sister were against him. In today's reading, we find Miriam and Aaron opposing Moses. They could not find fault with the way he was leading the people, so they started complaining about his wife. The fact was that Aaron and Miriam were jealous because God spoke to Moses more directly than to them.

What quality set Moses apart? "Now Moses was a very humble man, more humble than anyone else on the face of the earth" Numbers 12:3 (NLT). What a statement of character! God could use Moses because he was very humble. Miriam and Aaron did not understand that, so God did what every loving father would do to end the bickering, He said, "OK, the three of you, Aaron, Moses, and Miriam! I want you to come out to the Tent of Meeting!" So they went out—wouldn't you?

"Then God said, Miriam and Aaron I want you to step forward! . . . . Listen to My words: When a prophet of the Lord is among you, I reveal myself to Him in visions; I speak to him in dreams. But this is not true of my servant Moses; he is faithful in all My house. With him, I speak face to face, clearly and not in riddles, he sees the form of the Lord. Why then were you not afraid to speak against my servant Moses?" Numbers 12:7-9 (NIV). God was so angry with them that when His presence lifted from them, Miriam had leprosy. That is what you call a sound discipline from the Father!

Aaron then did an interesting thing. When he saw his sister's condition, he turned toward Moses, his brother, and said, "Oh, my lord, I beg you, do not account this sin to us, in which we have acted foolishly and in which we have sinned" Numbers 12:11 (NAS). What a compelling statement made from brother to brother! It was then that Moses cried out to God to have mercy on his sister. After a seven-day purification of abandonment from the camp, Miriam was healed of the leprosy. It took this intense sibling rivalry before Miriam and Aaron realized that God had set their brother Moses apart for a very special purpose.

Personal Note:

There are so many lessons in this passage of Scripture for me. God knew that Moses was His humble and willing servant. You would think that after all of the time that Aaron and Miriam were with Moses, after all of the miracles, after Moses meeting God on the mountain and God literally writing the ten commandments with His own finger, that they certainly would not question why God spoke to Moses and not them. However, just like any other children, jealousy got in the way and God had to step in and soundly punish them. If I had been in Miriam and Aaron's shoes, I would have been quivering and shaking to say the least!

My nature often gets in the way of God's perfect plan for me as well. When it does, God, like a loving Father, must correct me. Sometimes, very gently but when I do not listen, He has certainly had to "get my attention" a little more harshly. I am so glad that He is a loving Father and gives me His mercy as well!

Prayer:

Oh Father, how I long for You to call me, Your humble servant! I know that Your corrections can be harsh at times, but sometimes

that is the only way You can get my attention. Help me to be more open to Your will as You gently teach me to seek Your heart. In the precious name of Jesus, Amen.

Your Reflections:

Day 54

God is . . . The Appointment Maker

Bible Reading Jonah 1:11-17

How stubborn we can be when we want our own way, but God has something else in mind for us. Jonah is one of the examples that God gave us in the Bible, to show us that He is completely in control, no matter how much we fight against Him. It is sad that so often our willfulness can affect others as well.

Jonah did not want to go to Nineveh to give them the message that God wanted them to receive, because he did not like the people of Nineveh and did not want God to bless them. Therefore, he headed in the opposite direction, got on a boat to Tarshish, went below deck, and comfortably went to sleep. While he was asleep, a great storm came up and the sailors on the ship started throwing their cargo overboard in hopes of saving the ship and everyone who was boarded. Finally, the captain came down and woke up Jonah. After much agony, the men finally took Jonah's advice and they threw him overboard.

In Jonah, 1:17 we read, "And the Lord appointed a great fish to swallow up Jonah and Jonah was in the belly of the fish for three days and three nights." I chose this Revised Standard Version, because it said that God appointed a special fish to swallow Jonah. When I think about that, how powerful it is. Out of all of the sea, our sovereign God called one fish and told it to swallow Jonah. I am sure that during those three days, Jonah had plenty of time to repent of his waywardness.

The interesting thing is before God provided that fish, Jonah's actions caused the whole ship's crew to be affected by his rebellion. They lost their cargo; they feared for their lives and had to deal with their fear and responsibility of throwing a man overboard. Jonah wrote, "Then they (the men) cried out to the Lord, O Lord, please do not let us die for taking this man's life. Do not hold us accountable for killing an innocent man, for You, O LORD, have done as You pleased" Jonah 1:14 (NIV) (parenthesis mine). How often has my rebellious attitude toward my Father affected those around me? What a lesson for me!

Personal Note:

I wish I could say that I never am willful and want my own way. However, this is an area that my Father is working on within me. Whenever I am convicted of something, I know God wants to take me in a different direction, or perform something dissimilar within me. Yet even knowing this, sometimes I say, "No, God, I want to do it my way!" I do not literally say that, but by my ignoring the still small voice my silence speaks louder than words.

My heart is always heavy when I do this. It never brings me the happiness or satisfaction that I thought I wanted. Oh, how much I want to do His will in my life! He is teaching me, but it is a daily battle and that is what keeps me coming before Him so often throughout the day. I do know that I don't want Him to have to appoint something very drastic to get my attention. I want to learn to listen more intently to His ways.

Prayer:

Father, thank You for caring so much about me that You correct me when I do not listen to Your urgings. Help me to learn to pay attention to You more quickly! In Jesus' name, Amen.

Your Reflections:

Day 55

God is . . . The Talent Scout

Bible Reading: Exodus 35:30-35

The children of Israel had been in Egypt over 400 years and God continued to bless them and multiply them. However, a new Pharaoh came into power that had no knowledge of why the Israelites were in his nation. He became fearful, because they were so numerous—possibly, up to a couple of million people—so he made them all into slaves for his purposes. The work became extremely harsh and finally genocide was proposed. This Pharaoh wanted all newborn boys killed, but the midwives feared to do that and God protected them.

They had watched the mighty hand of The Almighty guide them and protect them. Nonetheless, they had gone through grievous sin against Him, and now it was time for Moses to give them the laws that God had given to him in the 40 days on Mt Sinai. God had already given precise directions about not only how to live, but how to build the Tabernacle in which the Lord would dwell and they would worship. He was very specific about every aspect from every garment that the priests would wear right down to the embellishments on their robes.

God was so detailed that at times, I have wondered where the talent came from to do such intricate work. After all, these people had not had any experience or schooling. They were used to hard labor, not creative and artistic work.

When it came time for God to show the people how to make all of the things for His holy tabernacle, Moses wrote about how God chose a man named Bezalel. In Exodus 31:3 (NIV) it reads, "and He has filled him with the Spirit of God with skills, ability and knowledge in all kinds of crafts" (NIV).

Further down in our reading it says that God chose a man named Oholiab to be his assistant. Exodus 31:6 (NIV). When we read about all of the things that needed to be made, we seldom think of how practical the Lord is in providing every tiny detail of our lives. We may think that we do not have talent but when we allow God to use us, He provides every skill and detail in whatever we need to carry out His plan. Two ordinary men with one extraordinary God!

Personal Note:

As I was reading this passage these verses just leaped off the page. I guess that is because of how He is using me right now. It brings me so much encouragement to know that I do not need a college degree in writing for God to use me. I do not need a major in anything except in obedience to whatever He wants to do in my life. What a blessing it is to know that the God of the universe will use any one of us and give us the talent and ability to fulfill His purpose. All we really need is willingness. The Almighty Talent Scout will do the rest!

Prayer:

Father, thank You for using just ordinary people so that I can be included. Make me ever willing to do whatever You have planned for my future as well as my present. How I appreciate You and honor You. In Jesus' name, Amen.

Your Reflections:

Day 56

God is . . . Our Baby Bloomer

Bible Reading: Hebrews 5:11-14

There is nothing that makes all heaven rejoice more than having a soul brought into the kingdom of God. To see a life reborn as it starts its Christian walk with Christ is magnificent. However, it is sad to see a Christian who has been reborn, but never gets past the very first stages of Christian growth.

Christ spoke often about being careful to make sure that our lives are ever growing in the knowledge and strength of our faith. One of the best-known parables that Jesus taught on spiritual growth was the farmer who planted seed. Each grain fell on different kinds of soil, but the good seed produced good crops. Matthew 13:8 puts it this way, "Still other seed fell on good soil. It came up, grew and produced a crop, multiplying thirty, sixty or even a hundred times" (NIV).

The Apostles' purpose for writing all of their work was to help us "bloom" as Christians. It is so sad sometimes to see a Christian blossom in faith but before the blossom is very full, it just stops growing and withers away. In our reading today, Paul talks about this in Hebrews 5:12 he wrote, "In fact, though by this time you ought to be teachers, you need someone to teach you the elementary truths of God's Word all over again. You need milk, not solid food" (NIV). I have been stagnant, and I have been in a period of growth. I can tell you, there is nothing like growth! It is exciting and a new page opening every day. I pray that I will not settle for less. Maturing in Christ is really the place I want to be!

Personal Note:

I lived in a dormant state in my Christian walk where I was content with living my life, but not having the Lord as my center. During this time, however, God was doing a lot of healing and working within me. I did not realize it at the time but looking back on it, I can now see how God never forgot me nor did I forget Him. I never lost my original faith but I wasn't really doing much to grow in my spiritual walk either. I was definitely in an unproductive state, where God was on the back burner and other things were occupying my time and my mind.

I was not bearing fruit. We are put here to bloom and blossom into mature Christians. That is where God wants us. Nonetheless, I have allowed God to begin to transform me into the person He created me to be. I am so thankful that He never let go of me. As I started to become obedient to His will, I started to grow. The tiny tender shoot of the beginning of spring began to produce tiny buds. I started to slowly open up and start to bloom. I found that I love blooming! I want to continue to blossom in Him, so that I will become the fruitful fragrance and sweet aroma that He created me to be. There is nothing more precious than that!

Prayer:

Father, thank You so much that You never let go of me. I praise You that as I continue to grow in Your grace and knowledge, that You will use me in ways that I could never even imagine. Oh how I love You! In Jesus' mighty name, Amen.

Your Reflections:

Day 57

God is . . . My Anger Release

Bible Reading: Job 32:1-5

We are living in a time where anger is very prevalent. It can be a very dangerous thing if we do not learn how to control it. With terror and violence all around us, and the busyness of our days becoming more and more stressful, it seems that people are finding it much harder to control their ravings.

Many people seem to become irate over almost anything. We find various examples of anger in Scripture, but our passage today shows a man ready to burst with his resentment. His name is Elihu. He was one of Job's friends. In five verses, Elihu's anger is mentioned three times.

He was the younger friend of Job, and out of respect, he kept silent while the three older friends talked to Job. "But when he saw that the three men had nothing more to say, his anger was aroused" Job 32:5 (NIV). Later in this chapter, verses 18-19 reads, "For I am full of words and the spirit within me compels me; inside I am like bottled up wine, like new wineskins ready to burst" (NIV).

Have you ever felt like that? You just knew that you could solve something, and no one would let you talk. You became very frustrated until you thought you would burst if you could not speak. You became so angry that when you finally did talk, you let the other person really "have it!" Proverbs 14:29 puts it like this, "Patient people have great understanding, but people with quick tempers show their foolishness" (NCV).

I have learned not to let things bottle up as often as I used to. Now I try to go right to my Father and say, "Father, help me. Keep me from speaking." Paul wrote, "Don't sin by letting anger control you. Don't let the sun go down while you are still angry, for anger gives a foothold to the devil" Ephesians 4:26-27 (NLT). Words spoken can never be taken back. I am so thankful that I am learning to go to my heavenly Father, sooner. He alone can keep me from acting foolish and being sorry for my words. He is my anger release valve.

Personal Note:

Most of the time when I get frustrated or angry, it is usually accompanied by a "pity party." Come to think of it, many times one triggers the other. I get hurt; I have a time of "poor me" and then I get angry. It is only as I let God take immediate control of the situation that I can calm down and get through whatever it may be without looking foolish. The amazing thing is, when He is in control, I feel victorious even in a situation when only moments before I might have felt defeated and hurt. He is the only real release I can go to no matter what the circumstances may be.

I had a situation just a couple of days ago that I turned directly over to Him. For a few seconds I wanted so much to speak, then His peace covered me, and I remained silent. Oh, how glad I was that He sheltered me from my own words!

Prayer:

Father, thank You for Your faithfulness and availability whenever I need You. Thank You for the victory that You bring into my life when I let You take control of any situation. I praise You and love You. In Jesus' name, Amen.

Your Reflections:

Day 58

God is . . . The Goal Completer

Bible Reading: Genesis 29:16-25

One of many great love stories in the Bible is the story of Jacob and Rachel. After deceiving His own brother, Jacob fled for his life and went to his mother Rebecca's family, to find solace and refuge. They lived a great distance away so Jacob lived with his mother's family. He fell in love with Laban's younger daughter, Rachel, and told his uncle Laban that he would work seven years for her hand in marriage. What a goal! What patience and love Jacob showed. Nevertheless, the day of marriage finally arrived, and Jacob was ecstatic that his goal was achieved.

He found out differently, however. In verse 25 it reads, "When morning came, there was Leah! So Jacob said to Laban, 'What is this you have done to me? I served you for Rachel, didn't I? Why have you deceived me?" (NIV). Leah was Rachel's older sister whoi was still unmarried.

There are many lessons in this story, but we remember Jacob's grandfather Abraham. God had promised him that he would be the father of many nations. Isaac his son had two sons. Now it was Jacob's turn and he had married the wrong sister! What happened to Jacob's dream? Had God forsaken him?

Jacob ended up working another seven years for Rachel, and he produced twelve sons, who became the children of Israel and multiplied just as God had promised.

Sometimes we have goals and dreams and it seems like we are in God's will, but we never know God's timing. The fulfillment of Abraham's goal was not completed in his lifetime, not even in Isaac's lifetime, but God prepared a defiant Jacob to bring about the tremendous growth and goal of his grandfather.

Exodus 1:6-7 states: "Now Joseph (Jacob's son) and all his brothers and all that generation died, but the Israelites were fruitful and multiplied greatly and became exceedingly numerous so that the land was filled with them" (NIV) (*parenthesis mine.*)

Personal Note:

Goal setting has always been a challenge. It brings some negative responses to me. Most of the time, my goals have been weight related goals—something I struggled with all my life. In my younger days, one of my ultimate aspirations was to have children.

God fulfilled that goal after several miscarriages and I have a wonderful son and daughter. In my later years, I went through a very dry period of my life when I was reaching toward different goals. Not that they were bad in themselves, but I don't think they were God's perfect plan for me.

It was not until I began to have the deep desire to know my Father more intimately that God began to accomplish one of the things that He had for me. Writing this devotional series is beyond my wildest expectation. The reason we are on this journey together is because over six years ago, I started desiring a closer relationship with God. Now not only do I have the goal of finishing this project, but also I can hardly wait to see what else He wants me to do for Him.

Like Jacob, I wanted things done my way and in my time frame, but God in His mercy and grace had so much more He wanted to do through me. How thankful I am that my Father sees everything and knows exactly what it will take to reach the objective that He has set for me. I can think of no higher calling than to meet the goals that God has for my life!

Prayer:

Father, thank You that You always know the goals we will accomplish in our lives. Help me to continue in patience and purpose to accomplish whatever You have set out for me to do. In Jesus name, Amen.

Your Reflections:

Day 59

God is . . . A Remaining Source

Bible Reading: Exodus 33:8-11

Remaining may seem like a strange quality, but it is one that takes patience and preparation. When we are learning a new job, it is rare for a new boss to just say to you, "This is your desk; this is your work now do it." You probably would be floundering around, thumbing through paperwork, trying to figure out the computer processes and many other things, without having any direction or input from someone who knew the job you were assigned.

Sometimes when we need to be thoroughly taught a skill, we need to remain with the person that can educate us on whatever it is that we must learn. If we are haphazard in this area, we can reap terrible consequences.

God is no different. Whenever He has something special to teach us, He wants us to remain with Him or with someone who can instruct us in what He needs us to learn. Joshua had been the constant companion of Moses and had been with Him through many of the miracles that God had performed. He could have taken for granted that he had been with Moses long enough and knew everything that made Moses tick.

However, in our reading today, we find an interesting passage. Remember the pillar of cloud? Whenever Moses went into the tent of meeting, God's presence in the pillar of cloud would come right down and hover at its entrance while the Lord talked to Moses. Whenever Moses would go out to the tent of meeting all the people would get up from whatever they were doing and go to the entrance of their own tents just to watch. Moses would enter the tent and literally talk to God.

In verse 11 we read, "Inside the Tent of Meeting, the Lord would speak to Moses face to face, as one speaks to a friend. Afterward Moses would return to the camp, but the young man who assisted him, Joshua son of Nun, would remain behind in the Tent of Meeting" (NLT). How interesting! No wonder that when it came time for Moses to go on to be with His God, Joshua was the prepared choice to lead the people. After all, he had much experience in "remaining!"

Personal Note:

I am learning to remain, also. When I remain in prayer and wait on my Father, He will always meet me and teach me. The periods of time when I become a bit impatient, unfocused and leave my prayer time before I really connect with Him, I feel that I am a little disoriented in my direction for the day. I need to remain and allow God to guide my day, so that there is order and calmness even through my busyness.

It really works! I can be interrupted, fielding phone calls, resolving whatever situation I need to handle, but if I have really met with my Father before I start my day, He brings order to my chaos. Remaining is definitely hard to do at times, but oh, so very rewarding!

Prayer:

Father, thank You for yet another lesson on relying on You for whatever I need. Help me to remain with You as You teach me what needs to be done during my day. Oh, the blessing You have for me when I listen intently to Your voice, and wait on You. How I praise You for Your grace each day. In Jesus' name, Amen.

Your Reflections:

Day 60

God is . . . Sovereign Omnipotence

Bible Reading: Daniel 2:31-38

The more we learn about God's sovereignty the more we understand His omnipotence. These two qualities of God go hand in hand. We see kingdoms rise and fall by the sweep of God's sovereign hand. He puts people in strategic places and in His perfect time, so that His overall purpose will be fulfilled.

We are living where we are today, because this is the time and place that God has appointed for us. If we truly understand His sovereign power, we will do everything we can to make sure that we are doing what He put us here to do. As we grow in Him, and become more familiar with His ways, we start to understand that each of us has an important spiritual purpose for living in this time and place.

King Nebuchadnezzar was not a "Christian" king. Yet God used him and his country to be the greatest and most strategic king in his time. God had given the king a very disturbing dream which none of his advisors could interpret. Through the threat of losing his life, Daniel and his three friends prayed for God's wisdom to interpret this dream. God granted Daniel's request and so much more. In Daniel 2:37 we read, "You, O king, are the king of kings. The God of heaven has given you dominion and power and might and glory" (NIV).

God would give the king all of this, and yet he put him through a trial of seven years that none of us would ever want to go through. The king went completely insane and lived like an animal on all four limbs, until he was able to acknowledge that God was the true and only God.

The almighty God of the universe used this way to humble King Nebuchadnezzar so that he would finally acknowledge God's power and sovereignty over His kingdom. Daniel 4:35 reads, "At the end of that time, I Nebuchadnezzar, raised my eyes toward heaven, and my sanity was restored. Then I praised the Most High; I honored and glorified Him who lives forever" (NIV). God does exactly what completes His purpose. He oversees everything that is going on! We may need to go through some humbling circumstances before we can acknowledge the sovereign omnipotence of our heavenly Father in our lives as well.

Personal Note:

It is such a wonderful thought to realize that God is at work everywhere at once. That means that He has His eye on my life as well as on our country and every person and nation in the world. As I ponder this phenomenon, it is so powerful! Even so, it is very comforting to me because I know that He literally has everything under control.

When I realize how His sovereign omnipotence affects me as a person, it brings a lot of stability, and also brings me to my knees in humble thanksgiving, because I know that I do not need to worry about anything that happens in my life, or anything that goes on in the world around me.

I am still in awe of all of the mighty and powerful things that God has done and continues doing in my life. I guess that is what I should expect from the One who made and keeps everything in total harmony, everyday and in every way, and still has time to count every hair on my head!

Prayer:

Father, thank You that You have Your eye and Your heartbeat on everything that goes on in the Universe. No matter what situation may arise, You are absolutely in control. Help me to continue learning from You as I walk one step at a time in Your power. In Jesus' name, Amen.

Your Reflections:

Day 61

God is . . . Satisfying

Bible Reading: Isaiah 26:2-8

What a wonderful thing it is to feel satisfied. It can be a fleeting event for us, but it also is something we continue to search for all of our lives. Many of us have sought satisfaction through fame, fortune, power, position, lust, alcohol and drugs. However, in this world, fulfillment seems to elude us.

There is really only one thing that can truly satisfy and that is an intimate relationship with our Father. God has created a vacuum within us that can only be fulfilled through Him because our very existence was created for Him. He wants a personal relationship with us, and only when we obey Him are we truly content.

Many of us, as Christians, live in that vacuum as well. Oh yes, we accept Christ as our Savior and that is good, but in order to receive God's best for us, we need to have more than just faith, we need a genuine confidence in knowing beyond any doubt that God is real and what He says He will do!

Satisfaction is talking to Him about everything in our lives—learning His will above our own. It is being confident that He genuinely cares about everything we do and knowing that He will do everything He promised in His Word. In verse 3 we read, "You will keep in perfect peace all who trust in You all whose thoughts are fixed on You" (NLT). Now that is real satisfaction!

Personal Note:

I don't know why as a human being it is so hard to just turn everything over to the Lord and trust Him completely. It seems that when I do that, something new comes into my life that I was not expecting and WHAM! I am trying to do things my way again!

If we have come from a background of being disappointed and deeply hurt by people in our lives, we naturally struggle more with trusting God. That is the case in my own life. It is difficult to imagine that God is trustworthy, when I have been disappointed and badly hurt by the people closest to me.

I am learning to trust my Father with my heart and when I do, He fills me with so much love and satisfaction that I overflow with thanksgiving and praise to Him. He is the only one who can bring me a steady and stable fulfillment that is lasting and complete.

I have been challenged a good part of my life with low self-esteem. I thought that I needed to look to someone else to make me happy or content. There is nobody else who can ever do that. I need to have enough confidence and worthiness within me to realize that God made me to be exactly who I am, and to look to Him to meet my need for contentment and satisfaction.

He always fulfills His end of the bargain and far beyond what I ever dreamed. It is a consistent abiding fullness that completes me in a way that nothing else ever can. It is a confidence in knowing that I am fearfully and wonderfully made and that I am a child of the King of the universe. The Psalmist wrote, "I will praise You, for I am fearfully and wonderfully made; marvelous are Your works, and that my soul knows very well" Psalm 130:14 (NKJ). No money can ever buy that kind of fulfillment. It is what my Father intended for me, from the day He formed me. He is complete satisfaction!

Prayer:

Father, How I praise You that You bring about a confidence within me that I could never have without You. You satisfy my every desire and add abundant peace and contentment to my

life. Thank You for bringing me to the place where I understand that You alone can make me complete. How I praise You! In the name of Jesus, Amen.

Your Reflections:

Day 62

God is . . . The Plumb Line of Righteousness

Bible Reading: Isaiah 28:14-17

Thoughts—how easy it is for our minds to listen to the negative messages our thoughts create every day. Often it is because we lack confidence or we cannot quite believe God's truth that makes it so easy to fall prey to the trap of believing a lie. This has been a personal challenge for me my entire life. It amazes me, because I love my Lord, and have read the Scripture as long as I can remember, but negative thoughts are very powerful.

One of the most powerful tools Satan uses is our thoughts. He loves to plant seeds of doubt, or fear in our minds. We might believe that God does not perform miracles today, that it was just something He did in the Bible. If we believe that, about the Bible then it diminishes the power and authority that God wishes to show through our lives. This is only one example of how easy it is for Satan to plant untruth into our thinking. On the other hand, God is truth! He cannot tell a lie, so either we trust what He said or we believe a lie.

His measurement is righteousness and justice and we can count on His Word as being the absolute truth. "Therefore this is what the Sovereign Lord says; Look! I am placing a foundation stone in Jerusalem, a firm and tested stone. It is a precious cornerstone that is safe to build on. Whoever believes need never be shaken. I will test you with the measuring line of justice; and the plumb line of righteousness" Isaiah 28:16, 17 (NLT). He never makes a promise that He does not keep. He will never say anything that He does not mean. He is the firm and tested cornerstone that we can build on, the fair measure and plumb line of righteousness. What a wonderful promise! We can always trust Him to tell us the truth

Personal Note:

How easy it is for me to limit God. All around, we are fed information daily that is just not the truth. I don't think it is always obvious. Satan is more subtle than that. He creates a half-truth so that we can buy into it. That is what he did with Eve in the Garden of Eden. Satan is so logical sometimes, that we do not stop and judge what the inner thought processes are saying. Is what I am hearing really God's word? Often times it is not. That is what creates doubt.

My desire is to listen more intently to the Holy Spirit's gentle voice allowing me to hear the truth above the drumbeat of Satan and my own insecurities. Whenever anything does not measure up to God's high standard of truth and righteousness, I want to be alert and say to my inner voice "No, that is a lie! Get behind me, Satan! Get out of my life." The more aware I am of what God's Word says, the easier it will be for me to stand against the inner voices of evil that seek to entrap me.

I am so thankful that God is much more powerful than Satan is; and I do not need to listen to Satan at all! However, in order to have complete victory I need to be strong in the knowledge of His Word and strong in prayer. I am very glad that I am growing in these areas. God is teaching me to trust Him so that I cannot be easily shaken!

Prayer:

Father, Your Word is truth. When I trust in it, I cannot be shaken. Help me to desire to learn more of You so that I can be prepared against the untruth that surrounds me daily. Keep me strong in You as I learn to trust You more. In Jesus' name, Amen.

Your Reflections:

Day 63

God is . . . Authority

Bible Reading: Luke 7:1-9

Jesus showed such deep mercy and power time after time in His ministry. People flocked to Him, always with their own agenda. Some wanted to be healed; some wanted to be fed, and some just wanted to watch Him and be with Him, so they could see the miracles that He performed. Few came humbly before Him. However, in all the self-absorption of the masses, Jesus found only a small number of people who really understood who He was and what they were asking of Him.

One of those was the Roman Centurion, who valued his servant so much that he sent for Jesus to come and heal him. He was a man used to giving and taking orders. He had high regard for authority and Jesus knowing this, went with them. "He (Jesus) was not far from the house when the centurion sent friends to say to Him, Lord, don't trouble Yourself, for I do not deserve to have You come under my roof. That is why I did not even consider myself worthy to come to You. But say the word, and my servant will be healed" Luke 7:6-8 (NIV) Parenthesis mine).

How refreshing it must have been for Jesus to have someone who understood how authority works and understood His position. After all, the man was high in earthly authority, yet humble enough to realize that there was a far greater authority at work here. "When Jesus heard this, He was amazed at him, and turning to the crowd following Him, He said, 'I tell you, I have not found such great faith even in Israel'" Luke 7:9 (NIV). The Centurion believed so

160

strongly that He was able to say, "Jesus, just speak a word and I know my servant will be healed!" Of course, Jesus healed the servant. Such confidence! That much faith generates healing power! How awesome!

Personal Note:

Jesus told us in the Scripture; "I tell you the truth, if you have faith as small as a mustard seed, you can say to this mountain, Move from here to there and it will move. Nothing will be impossible for you!" Matthew 17: 20-21 (NIV).

I think that my faith is strong, but when I compare it to what is available to me it is minuscule! Most of us cannot even grasp the power and authority that we have in Christ Jesus. As I ponder this, I know that I do not yet comprehend all the authority that I have available to me. In Matthew 28:18 (NIV) just before Jesus ascended up into heaven, He said, "All authority in heaven and on earth has been given to me." He wants us to model our ways after Him, so that means that I have all His authority at my beck and call! How powerful! How compelling! Oh, how I seek to grasp such a convincing truth!

Prayer:

Father, teach me about the authority that I have available to me through You, when I believe. Increase my desire to learn more of You that I may grow in power and might according to Your promise. Strengthen my faith. In Jesus' powerful name, Amen.

Your Reflections:

Day 64

God is . . . The Giver of Mercy

Bible Reading: Luke 23:32-33, 39-43

Jesus, the giver of mercy, was shown no mercy. He was made to carry His own cross on which He would be crucified. He was nailed to that cross after a nightmarish day and night, then He was rejected, mocked, accused, beaten to a pulp, scorned and had a crown of thorns crushed onto His head. You would think with all of that, there would be nothing left for Him to give to others, let alone show mercy, but He did! He looked down at His mother, and then He asked John the disciple to care for her from then on.

One of the best examples of His mercy was to one of the thieves crucified with Him. He wanted us to know that no matter how late in the game that we seek Him, He is always ready to receive us into His family. Many seek that mercy as they cry out on their deathbed, "Lord be merciful to me, a sinner." Sometimes that person has not been a good person in life. We hear of people in prison accepting Christ as their Savior after committing heinous crimes. At times, it is hard for us to imagine a heaven that will hold criminals in the same light as "we" who are so good! God said, "All our righteousness is as filthy rags to Him" Isaiah 64:6b (NLT).

There are so many examples in Christ's ministry on earth. His mercy reached into the depths of our fleshly nature to pick up prostitutes, adulterers, financial cheaters, a son who exhausted his inheritance on all of the sin the world had to offer, and many more.

Nevertheless, on the cross His love and mercy was extended to a criminal who was on a cross right beside Him. One of the thieves spoke to the other one who was insulting Christ and said, "We are punished justly, for we are getting what our deeds deserve. But this man has done nothing wrong. Then he said to Jesus, 'Remember me when You come into Your kingdom.' Jesus answered him, 'I tell you the truth, today you will be with Me in paradise'" Luke 23:41-43 (NKJ). Jesus was happy to be merciful to a heart that sought Him. He will be merciful to us as well. It does not matter what we have done! How marvelous is our God!

Personal Note:

I have never been one who was resentful because a murderer who accepts Christ as his Savior will go to the same heaven as I do. I have always felt the weight of my own sin—sometimes too heavily. My nature has had trouble receiving forgiveness when I erred, even though I knew that Jesus had already forgiven me for my sin. Even now, I carry that load at times, but God is helping me build confidence by understanding that He paid the price for whatever burden I bear.

I am learning that I can never let my Savior down, or sin in any way that has not already been paid for at the high cost of Christ's death on the cross. For me to be self-centered enough to keep feeling bad about any given failure is not what God wants for me. It really is taking away the power of the cross and trying to carry it again myself! That is the sin of unbelief and disobedience, no matter how I would like to sugarcoat it.

His mercy is so deep and His grace so strong that I do not need to carry any burden in my life. I am a long way from having complete victory over this, but I have grown and can hardly wait for the day that I will instantly give something over to Him without a moment's worry or concern. There is such freedom available to me if I only accept Christ's mercy, only believe, and turn it over to Him. After all, that is what mercy is all about!

Prayer:

Father, Thank You for such mercy that You have already forgiven me of every wrong that I will ever do in my life. Help me to remember that the burden is not mine. You bought it with Your blood and Your mercy covers it. How I praise You, my merciful Lord! Amen.

Your Reflections:

Day 65

God is . . . Prepared

Bible Reading: 2 Chronicles 14:1-7

During the reign of all of the kings of Judah, there were some who trusted in our living God and some who defied Him. Abijah had ruled in Judah and trusted in our God, and one of the saddest stories of the kings, for me, is when Abijah had to go to war against his brothers in Israel. God brought judgment on Jeroboam king of Israel. God allowed Abijah to win over his brother's country of Israel, because Abijah cried out to God to help him.

This victory was not lost on Abijah's son, Asa, and when Abijah died, Asa was a young man. The Scripture says, "Asa did right in the sight of God," and God allowed a decade of peace, while He was preparing Asa for His plan and purpose. Nevertheless, Asa was like many of us today. He became complacent and too comfortable. As he grew older, God was not as important to him as He once was. God allowed an Ethiopian army of one million men to come against Judah. Asa came to his senses and cried out to God to help him. God allowed a miraculous victory for Judah.

After a thirty-five year reign of relative peace, Asa started to rely more on himself again and less on God. A prophet was sent to him from God to correct him. Asa flew into a rage and had the prophet put in prison.

We read this sad commentary, "In the thirty-ninth year of his reign, Asa developed a serious foot disease. Yet even with the severity of his disease, he did not seek the Lord's help but turned only to his physicians. So he died in the forty-first year of his reign" 2 Chronicles 16:12, 13 (NLT). How sad! God had prepared him to be a great king and he had so much potential; but in the end, he died because he did not ask God for help. What parallels there are for us today. God wants us to be prepared. Will we ask Him for help or will we rely on someone else? He is waiting for our reply.

Personal Note:

I have learned, I hope, a huge lesson in this story. What a question it raises in my own heart. Am I ready to rely on God to prepare me for whatever comes my way, or do I still want to try to do things in my own strength?

Sometimes my heart says one thing but my actions show another. God has a rich life in store for me. However, it may take some very hard preparation, some deep valleys and rough road. There may be a huge army ready to come against me. Will I cry out to my Father for His help, or will I take the matter into my own hands and ignore Him? My desire is to fall on my face humbly before Him, and cry out for His help and strength as He is in the process of preparing me for His plan and purpose in my future.

Prayer:

Father, prepare the way for Your potential in my life. Make me willing to endure the preparation and fill me with Your strength, Your grace and Your peace. I humble myself before You, for You alone can bring about Your purpose in my life. In Jesus' name, Amen.

Your Reflections:

Day 66

God is . . . Divine Guidance

Nehemiah 9:16-21

Ezra lived in a very critical time for Israel. After Babylon had destroyed the temple and had taken the Jews captive, along came Persian rule. God was with the Persian King, Cyrus, who allowed the Jews to go back to Jerusalem and rebuild their temple. However, when the enemies of the Jews tried to help this group rebuild the temple, the people saw right through them and refused to let them help. These enemies mingled with the people and began to plant seeds of doubt and fear and after a while, the builders became discouraged and quit. However, God's purpose had not yet been fulfilled.

After King Cyrus, came Darius and then King Xerxes. You might remember the name of King Xerxes. He married Queen Esther and God guided her to help free His people from a terrible plot to annihilate all of the Jews.

This laid the groundwork for the next king, Artexerxes who helped send another group of Jews back to Jerusalem under the ministry of Ezra, who was a scribe and priest and a quiet godly man. "For Ezra had devoted himself to the study and observance of the law of the Lord, and to teaching its decrees and laws in Israel" Ezra 7:10 (NIV). Ezra brought worship and knowledge back to the people.

However, God was not through guiding His people. There was a cupbearer of King Artexerxes named Nehemiah. He was a type "A" personality, who had a deep longing to go back to Jerusalem and rebuild the walls of the city. He was a "let's-get-it-done right" type of guy and under his leadership, despite many obstacles, he was able to accomplish what God wanted done, but it took months of fasting and prayer before he was ready to take on this mighty task for his God.

Nehemiah wrote, "But You are a forgiving God, gracious and compassionate, slow to anger and abounding in love" Nehemiah 9:17 (NIV). No matter how many times the people rejected God; He always guided them back to the right path. He does the same for us, today. God is our divine guide and when we listen, He brings us back into His purpose, leads and directs us no matter what the obstacle. What a merciful God!

Personal Note:

I recently had a situation where I got ahead of God's plan. I was on the right course; I just jumped ahead of His timing. What I had to learn was that I need His preparation and direction before He can guide me into His master plan.

The idea that He gave me after my little "glitch" was so much better than anything I could ever come up with on my own. He is a fabulous guide when I follow His lead, and not try to get ahead of His guidance.

Prayer:

Father, You alone can direct my life and perform Your perfect will in me. Help me to wait for Your divine guidance in my life. Help me to seek You first before I jump ahead of Your perfect timing. In Jesus' name, Amen.

Your Reflections:

Day 67

God is . . . The Gift That Gives

Bible Reading: Luke 2:8-14

At the time of this writing, we are starting into the holiday season where we think about buying gifts for family members and friends. It can be a very joyful period or a real frustration. We have moved a long way from the days of the pioneer mother who would work diligently to make a homemade rag doll that a little girl would cherish the rest of her life, or a simple truck that the father would make out in the barn with left over wood. We now live in a world of give me more and more and many children are disappointed if they do not get everything on their list.

The greatest gift of all was given to us by the Father. He gave His Son, Jesus Christ, who was not born in a mansion but a manger. He was not sought after, but His parents sought after a place for Him to be born. He was not visited by thousands, but by lowly shepherds who came to worship Him. He should have been known by all, but most rejected Him. One innkeeper had mercy on Him and offered a stable for His birth. Few recognized that He was someone special, but those who did received a blessing that was life changing.

Among them was Simeon, who had waited and looked for the Lord's appearing his whole life, and Anna, a widow who never left the temple but prayed continuously for her Messiah to come. God richly blessed Simeon and Anna and allowed them to know that they were seeing the Messiah whom they had looked forward to for so long.

The majority of us today live our busy daily lives barely giving a thought to this precious gift. On Sunday before Christmas, as we prepare to go to our individual places of worship, we may start thinking about Him. However, even there we may be too busy serving Him to think about who He truly is. We look at the crosses in our churches and say a few words in prayer to Him, and then go back to our busy lives and miss the greatest blessings of the Father, because we are too busy to receive them.

That day, over 2000 years ago, Simeon gave his gift back to his Messiah, when he said in Luke 2:30-32, "For my eyes have seen Your salvation, which You have prepared in the sight of all people, a light for revelation to the Gentiles and for glory to Your people Israel" (NIV). May we not forget God's gift of His Son who gave the ultimate gift to us when He died for us. He is the gift that keeps giving!

Personal Note:

I have to admit that this is the busiest time of the year for me. However, I have learned to appreciate the gift of our Savior who was born with such humble beginnings. He never forgot His humility, or the Father who sent Him to earth to pay the price for our sins. I honor Him and want to keep His gift of salvation before me as I move into this time.

With thanksgiving and praise, I thank Him for receiving me into His kingdom where I have so much waiting for me. While I am here on earth, my reward is to be with family and friends during this busy time and to remember my Savior who gave me the ultimate gift!

Prayer:

Father, I pray that I will remember this season, Your greatest gift of all, May I give back to You a gift of gratitude for Your Son who

gave continually and then paid the price so that I might be a part of Your kingdom forever. How I thank You for Your great love and mercy. In my Savior's name, Amen

Your Reflections:

Day 68

God is . . . Possessor of Healing Wings

Bible Reading: Malachi 4:1-3

I have always liked the way that artists portray angels. Their wings are magnificent. They are usually portrayed with purity and a featherlike quality. I am sure that reality is so much more beautiful than anything our minds can conjure up, but it is a wonderful image. Stores are filled with images of angels. Some with fiber-optic lighting that gives them an extra ethereal glow. Galleries display the majestic creations of artists' paintings of powerful angels flying with glorious wings.

Isaiah portrayed the vision he saw of angels, "Attending him were mighty seraphim, each having six wings. With two wings, they covered their faces. With two they covered their feet, and with two they flew" Isaiah 6:2 (NLT). What an exquisite picture this portrays. However, if angels are so ethereal, I cannot even imagine what God's wings must be like.

The Psalmist wrote, "Keep me as the apple of Your eye; hide me in the shadow of Your wings" Psalm 17:8 (NLT). God's wings must be huge and immensely powerful, if we only need to be in the shadow of them to find a place of safety and solace. His wings provide a covering to keep us safe from our enemies.

As we approach the end of this age, where violence and terror are ever increasing and our world is turned upside down and wrong side out, it is such a comfort to know that God has a promise for us.

In our reading today, Malachi talks about God's wings. "But for you who revere My name, the Sun of Righteousness will rise with healing in its wings. And you will go free, leaping with joy like calves released from the stall" Malachi 4:2 (NIV). He will be like the healing warmth of the sun to us who love and obey Him and live righteously before Him. We will become carefree and lighthearted just like baby animals that frolic around without worry or care. What a warm cozy picture this presents. What a comfort this brings to my soul.

Personal Note:

The stresses of life can be very heavy at times. Even without worrying about our world, just our everyday life can be very challenging. I am so grateful that Christ will cover me with His glorious wings and protect me from the hurts and hard places of everyday life. He has done that for me countless times.

Whenever something comes into my life that is very difficult to understand, I come to Him for His calming presence and I know that He will cover me with His mighty wings, and I will be safe from harm. He has never failed me. All I have to do is trust Him with the situation. There is healing in those marvelous wings! What confidence that brings to my heart!

Prayer:

Father, Thank You for Your mighty wings that are a shelter and a healing for me in time of need. Thank You for always being available to me, to heal my hurts and my pain. In Christ's magnificent name, Amen.

Your Reflections:

Day 69

God is . . . A Heart Surgeon

Bible Reading: Psalm 51:1-13

I am amazed at the timing of this one! The Lord has really been working within me and cleansing me in so many ways, but I am still a cracked vessel in some areas. My number one struggle has always been a weight problem. As the Lord fashions me into His image, I am having such a struggle turning this one exclusively over to Him. Why is that? Is it because I have not submitted this area to Him without conditions attached? I still allow my fleshly nature, which is Satan's domain, to manipulate me.

Like David, I have sinned against the Lord. I reread the first paragraph and I can see where my sin lies. I used the words "struggle, problem, hard time." I need to allow the Lord to perform surgery on my heart. I do not understand the struggle, yet I know if I want to be His completely, I must yield this area over to Him. The psalmist wrote, "For I know my transgression and my sin is always before me. Against You, You only, have I sinned and done what is evil in Your sight" Psalm 51:3-4 (NIV).

Yes, God is using His scalpel on me and will continue to do so until I am entirely purged. Then I can become more effective for Him. I know that it will be a daily fight against the "hold" that Satan and my own will has in this area, but as I sincerely allow God to pierce my heart and perform His surgery, I know there will be healing in store for me.

Right now, I am on step one of the process. Verse 6 gives me instruction as to what my heart attitude must be. David wrote, "Surely You desire truth in the inner parts; You teach me wisdom in the inmost place" (NIV). Then we get to the wonderful verse that many of us have memorized. "Create in me a pure heart, O God, and renew a steadfast spirit within me" Psalm 51:10 (NIV). That steadfast spirit is absolutely what I need. I know He is ready and waiting to provide it!

Personal Note

As I bear my soul and my sin before you, through this writing, I know that God is just waiting for me to turn this area over to Him for His surgery. I am going to print this Day 69, which I wrote on November 23, 2006, and read it often as a reminder that He alone can heal this part of my being; and I am marking this day as the beginning of a new understanding of His desire for me.

Food was always a treat as I grew up, and a way to solve my pain and hurts. I probably have been on most every diet and weight program invented, and have spent thousands of dollars on a variety of quick fixes over my lifetime. Nothing has ever worked permanently. I have tried to turn my weight problem over to my Lord but have been unsuccessful there as well. Our habits can be a huge stronghold in our lives.

I want to yield and give God my obesity and pray, "Please Father take this burden on You and give me rest. "Come to Me, all you who are weary and burdened, and I will give you rest. Take my yoke upon you and learn from Me, for I am gentle and humble in heart, and you will find rest for your souls. For my yoke is easy and my burden is light" Matthew 11:28-30 (NIV).

It is now 2012 and my body has not changed very much. What the Lord has done, however, is to take away the guilt and burden I was carrying about this issue and the Holy Spirit is always faithful to give me gentle nudges to make healthier decisions. I give my Lord full praise for His faithfulness. He has filled me with peace that has replaced the constant fretting. I would love to have a thinner body but nothing will ever replace the inner joy that can only come from a heart yielded to Him!

Prayer:

Father, please help me to be a testimony of Your forgiveness, grace and mercy as I publicly bring this area of my life to light. Help all who are struggling with addictions and obsessions that they may have the courage to step out in faith and give them to You for Your healing. In Jesus' mighty name, Amen.

Your Reflections:

Day 70

God is . . . Purity

Bible Reading: Philippians 4:4-9

"Blessed are the pure in heart, for they will see God" Matthew 5:8 (NIV). Jesus said those words in His sermon on the mount. If you have never read this inspiring passage, I encourage you to do so. Matthew, chapters five, six and seven are the roadmap for living a Christ-like life and receiving every blessing that He has for us. Purity is one quality that is completely a "God" quality.

I received an email from a friend who used quotes to compare life today to life in the year 1955, just over fifty years ago. Here are a few of them.

"Kids today are impossible! Those sideburns and ducktail haircuts make it impossible to stay groomed. Next thing you know, boys will be wearing their hair as long as the girls."

"I'm afraid to send my kids to the movies any more. Ever since they let Clark Gable get by with saying a swear word in 'Gone with the Wind,' it seems every new movie has one in it."

"More and more girls are getting their ears pierced. If God had intended for us to do that, He would have made holes in our ears"

"Marriage doesn't mean a thing any more; those Hollywood stars seem to be getting divorced at the drop of a hat!"

We definitely have gone downhill in purity since then! The 1960's ushered in immorality and disrespect. It has been on a very slippery slope since then. Left to ourselves, we will always go away from purity, not toward it.

Paul was so convinced of this truth that he told us in Philippians exactly how we need to process our thoughts, as well as our actions! "Finally brothers, whatever is true, whatever is noble, whatever is right, whatever is pure, whatever is lovely, whatever is admirable—if anything is excellent or praiseworthy—think about such things" Philippians 4:8 (NIV).

Personal Note:

How rich my life is when my thoughts are pure. When I am righteously following Christ's example, I will not be having judgmental opinions, no tempting little white lies to tell, I will be thinking good thoughts about everyone. That is where I want to be in relationship with Him, because these are a few of the things that if I am not watchful and in tune with His urgings, can rob me of my purity. Keeping my mind consistently under His rule—is one goal that I want to achieve.

Since we are all human, I am not sure that any of us can ever achieve perfection in this, but we can reach out to live the kind of life that embraces purity. I am not talking about being a "stuffed shirt" or never having fun. I am talking about living my life so that my thoughts are under the complete guidance of my Father.

Every area that I can turn over to Him is one step closer to reaching the high mark that He has set for me. How my heart yearns for that! Reaching toward the mark and not turning back is my ultimate goal.

Prayer:

Thank You, Father, for always speaking to my heart. Thank You for showing me the many areas in which I need to trust

You. Help me to continue to reach toward Your high calling as I learn to walk in more purity day by day. In my Savior's name, Amen.

Your Reflections:

Day 71

God is . . . Childlike

Bible Reading: Mark 10:13-16

Recently I went to a women's seminar at our church. It was so much fun. We had our worship service, and then we were told to go downstairs to our multi-purpose room because something special was prepared for us to do. As we sat down, we noticed that each place had a cloth square and in the center of the table were marking pens, stamps, and other crafty things.

We were then asked to take that blank piece of cloth and decorate it with something that reflected our theme, "Bloom Where You Are Planted." You could hear grumbling all around the room as women young and old tried to figure out what they wanted to do or even if they could do it. In the end, we really had some unique squares, which the church was going to put together and make a quilt to donate to a family in need.

I could not help but think if this same project was given to a group of four or five year olds, how awesome and creative they would have been, without grumbling or complaining. Each child would bring uninhibited creativity to the project.

As adults, we bury the beautiful creativity that God intended for us to have and use freely, because our insecurities and self-restraints block the freedom we had as children. As a result, we are so caught up in our "stuff" that it is hard for us to understand and accept the simple things of His kingdom.

Jesus talked about this to His disciples, as people were bringing their little children to Him to be healed. The disciples were trying to prohibit them from bothering Jesus. Maybe the day had been long and hard and they were protecting Him. The Scripture really doesn't say, but Jesus was indignant and He said, "Let the little children come to me and do not hinder them, for the kingdom of God belongs to such as these" Mark 10:14 (NIV).

Personal Note:

My daughter, Jill, came to visit us in Oregon the day after Thanksgiving. Saturday our son, daughter-in-law and grandson came over to spend some time with her, and have a great family day together. Jill had bought a gingerbread house kit to assemble. My four-and-a-half year old grandson was enamored by the process. I helped some, but mostly I sat just watching his face beaming with joy as he helped Aunt Jill build this gingerbread house. His imagination and creativity were displayed so vividly. I cannot help but feel how much we miss by "growing up." The childlike wonder and appreciation of what their young minds are able to conjure up is so incredible!

That is how God wants us to be about His kingdom. He loves us to have awe and wonder about everything that He says, does, and can do. I am very grateful that He is teaching me just that. Slowly, I am opening up to Him, like a new bud opens its tender leaves to the sun and comes into bloom in the fullness of spring. I can hardly wait for His next lesson for me!

Prayer:

Father, thank You for teaching me to become more childlike. I want everything about You to be fresh and new as I continue on Your path, ever closer to Your heart. In Jesus' Name, Amen.

Your Reflections:

Day 72

God is . . . Generously Creative

Bible Reading: Psalm 104:10-15

The earth is full of God's praise! I feel especially blessed to live in the Willamette Valley, in Oregon because it is very rich and verdant. All nature is alive and flourishing most of the year. However, I love the winter as well.

We do not have snow here very often, maybe two or three events a year; and many years it does not stick. This year, however, we had an early snow. Our daughter, Jill, was visiting from Phoenix, Arizona, and we awoke up to a winter wonderland. We were both extremely excited and we stayed home for a couple of days just taking in God's wonder.

The Psalmist has so much to say about God's creation. Everything in nature is alive. David wrote Psalm after Psalm to remind us of how luxuriant and prosperous our Creator made everything.

"He causes the grass to grow for the cattle, and vegetation for the service of man, that he may bring forth food from the earth, and wine that makes glad the heart of man, oil to make his face shine, and bread which strengthens man's heart. The trees of the Lord are full of sap, the cedars of Lebanon which He planted. Where the birds make their nests, the stork has her home in the fir trees" Psalm 104:14-18 (NKJ). Our Father is so generous with us. He has given the earth and all its riches to us that we may thrive and grow strong not only in body, but also in spirit, as well.

Another thing that struck me about this passage was that the stork has her home in the fir trees. Now I know quite a bit about fir trees. We have many of them, but I think if I looked up into a fir tree and saw a stork, that would be worth seeing!

We have wild turkeys here. They fly straight up and find their rest at the top of oak trees. It is quite a sight to see these huge birds way up high in the trees, sleeping. How beautifully God provides every detail for every living thing! "O Lord, what a variety of things You have made. In wisdom, You have made them all. The earth is full of Your creatures" Psalm 104:24 (NLT). He truly makes our planet thrive with His goodness and care.

Personal Note:

I wrote the following while my daughter and I were snowed in, "I looked out my front door this morning to a beautiful carpet of white snow covering every blade of grass. The branches of the trees, empty of their leaves, brought a lacy white brilliance as each snowflake fell gently to the earth. It reminded me that God has not made any two snowflakes alike. Each is unique unto itself. God knew exactly the number of flakes that would blanket my little world."

Winter or summer, autumn or spring, God brings all nature alive and flourishing with His bounty. "He waters the hills from His upper chambers; the earth is satisfied with the fruit of Your works" Psalm 104:13 (NLT). "Bless the Lord, O my soul! and all that is within me bless His holy name!" Psalm 103:1 (NLT).

Prayer:

Father, how marvelous You are in all Your ways. I praise You for every thing that flourishes under Your abundant care. You truly are an awesome God. Thank You, In Jesus' name, Amen.

Your Reflections:

Day 73

God is . . . Our Divine Council

Bible Reading: Exodus 18:17-23

Have you ever overworked? A job had to be accomplished in a given time, and you did it all yourself even though there were competent people who could have helped? I think we all have done that at one time or another.

Moses found himself in this situation. He had been the only counsel to all of the children of Israel, and it was an incredibly heavy load. He never complained, but God knew and sent Moses' father-in-law, Jethro, at just the right time to help. "Moses listened to his father-in-law and did everything he said. He chose capable men from all Israel and made them leaders of the people, officials over thousands, hundreds, fifties and tens" Exodus 18:24-25 (NIV).

He was not afraid to take the wise counsel of this intelligent man and willingly turn over the responsibility to competent men within the Israelite tribes. Numbers 12:3 (NIV) tells us how God viewed Moses, "Now Moses was a very humble man, more humble than anyone else on the face of the earth." He was quick to take God's advice, and he was just as open to taking his father-in-law's advice.

We are not always as quick to listen to constructive criticism. Many times our ego gets in the way. We have then lost the chance to allow someone else the joy and growth of doing something for us.

God is our divine counsel. We do not like it any better when He lets us know that we are not as important as we think we are. That

184

is called arrogance. What makes us think that we know better than the God who created us? Yet, we go about life trying to struggle through and "do it ourselves" when God has a much easier and wiser plan for us.

Taking someone else's advice can be a challenge to our egos. Proverbs 15:33 reads: "The fear of the Lord teaches a man wisdom, and humility comes before honor" (NIV). Becoming humble and accepting advice from both God and man is a goal that is really worth reaching.

Personal Note:

When I read about God's evaluation of Moses as being the most humble man on the face of the earth, I thought, what an enormous statement! I wonder, if I could see what God would inscribe about me. What would He say? High on my priority list of things I would like on that statement from my Father would be that I was humble and willing to seek His counsel as well! I would also love Him to write that I am a woman after His own heart. Listening to His divine counsel is the only one that will matter in the end!

Prayer:

Father, continue to work Your work in my life that I might be able to listen to Your wise counsel. Help me to come before You in the quiet, that I might hear Your voice more clearly. In Jesus' name, Amen.

Your Reflections:

Day 74

God is . . . Our Hope

Bible Reading: Romans 8:18-25

Hope is like a candle flame that never burns out. No matter how tough our lives become, there is that tiny flame of hope that can flicker at times, but it never goes completely dark. Without a tiny flicker of hope, our lives are meaningless.

God has created in everyone a glimmer of hope. Genesis tells us that even nature has hope. "Against its will, all creation was subjected to God's curse. But with eager hope, the creation looks forward to the day when it will join God's children in glorious freedom from death and decay" Romans 8:20, 21 (NLT).

When did that happen? It was when Adam and Eve sinned. They lived in a perfect environment until that day. Can we even imagine what it was like to look at a daffodil, or a lily, or a rose blooming; and the blooms never faded, withered and died? That is what it was like before sin came into the world. When God initiated the curse on Adam and Eve, it included the earth as well.

"And to the man He said, Since you listened to your wife and ate from the tree whose fruit I commanded you not to eat, the ground is cursed because of you. It will grow thorns and thistles for you, though you will eat of its grains. By the sweat of your brow will you have food to eat until you return to the ground from which you were made" Genesis 3:17-19. (NLT).

Even in the curse, God left hope for Adam and Eve. Along with the curse came provision and mercy. "So the Lord God banished them from the Garden of Eden, and He sent Adam out to cultivate the ground from which He had been made" Genesis 3:23 (NLT).

How dreadful Adam and Eve must have felt when their life of perfection spiraled into their new reality. Adam had to live for the rest of his life looking at nature all around him, realizing how perfect everything used to be. Now, because of their sin everything was cursed.

However, God put His stamp of approval on them by providing them with a family, which was a blessing and a curse. Life will always be a blessing and a curse because that is what life is all about. Nonetheless, in all of that, we have a glimmer of hope to reach deep inside ourselves and allow our Father to help us go through the times of brokenness and anguish.

Timothy talks about this hope. "This is why we work hard and continue to struggle, for our hope is in the living God, who is the Savior of all people and particularly of all believers" I Timothy 4:10 (NLT).

Personal Note:

Hope has been my constant companion all through my life. In fact, I have used that word often. I am always being hopeful about something. Hope is that little nudge deep inside me that generates my dreams and ambitions. It directs my achievements, aspirations and confidence. Hope motivates my belief, faith, expectation and my trust—it is everything positive.

When I hope, I send negative feelings and thoughts running. Hope deepens my confidence in knowing that Christ dwells within me, and that I have a bright future awaiting me in His kingdom. What an amazing gift God gives me in hope! Of that, I am confident!

Prayer:

Father, thank You for the gift of hope. We are all created with it. My hope is in You, Lord. You are all I need. Help me to keep hope alive and strong, as I trust You each day, by faith. In Jesus' name, Amen.

Your Reflections:

Day 75

God is . . . Sustainer of Vitality

Bible Reading: Psalm 92:12-16

Vitality is created from the green meadows and peaceful waters that God gives us. They last us a lifetime. Green is the very symbol of life and peace to me. It is to my Father as well. One of the beloved Psalms that most of us have memorized, at least in part, is the 23rd, "He lets me rest in green meadows; He leads me beside peaceful waters" Psalm 23:2 (NLT). I used this version, because the picture it creates in my mind is so vivid. Some versions say, "He makes me lie down in green pastures. He leads me beside still waters." God's best for us is to experience this; because in His rest is where we regain our strength and vitality as well.

Another Psalm that I have read many times, but it did not "click" with me until I heard a sermon preached on it, is our reading today. "But the godly will flourish like palm trees and grow strong like the cedars of Lebanon. For they are transplanted in the Lord's own house. They flourish in the courts of our God. Even in old age they will still produce fruit, they will remain vital and green" Psalm 92:12-15 (NLT).

The palm trees of the Middle East are mostly date palms. Dates are a staple fruit in that region. A couple of interesting facts about these wonderful trees are that, they are endogen, which means that they grow from within and their best and sweetest fruit is produced in old age.

That is so like the Father. He tells us that the older we get the more fruit we can produce and the "best" fruit, at that! The older we get the more vital and fruitful we become, because we grow from within. He loves us so much that just when the fruit is at its peak of ripeness, He transplants us into His own courts of heaven. "Even in old age they will still produce fruit; they will remain vital and green" Psalm 92:14 (NLT). Yes, heaven is full of beautiful old palm trees . . . God's choice trees that have matured and been full of the sweetness of service in His kingdom! I can hardly wait!

Personal Note:

When we look around at churches, we mostly see young people working the hardest for God's kingdom. Many older Christians feel like they have done their share, now it is time to allow the "younger folks" to do the work. It is good to know that God has a plan for us even in our old age. He wants us to grow stronger, more vital and greener as we mature.

My personal journey, I feel, is just beginning. I want to be more effective for Him than ever before. Scripture teaches us that the old should teach the young, because we have a lifetime of wisdom that we have learned through the "college" of hard knocks!

I may serve Him differently as I grow older, but my desire is to continue to serve Him in any way that He wants to use me. I am eager to pass on some of the "sweet fruit" that I have learned through living and growing from the inside. I guess that is why, as a senior citizen of God's kingdom, I do not feel older inside.

Just the mortal body is decaying. God's vitality and fresh green meadows are verdant and blooming with a sweetness that only comes with mature fruit for His kingdom. Lord willing, I will still be bearing fruit until the day that He transplants me into His heavenly courts!

Prayer:

Father, You are so remarkable! Your blessings are so rich to me! How I want to produce sweet ripe fruit for Your kingdom.

Help me never to be satisfied to just sit in a pew and let younger people do what You have called me to do. In Your precious name, Jesus! Amen.

Your Reflections:

Day 76

God is . . . My Ultimate Catharsis

Isaiah 1:18-20

We often see detergent commercials that promise us a deeper clean than what we are currently using. It seems that there is a new product on the market continually promising more than the last one. Whether it is for our clothes, faces or our hair, everyone wants to get us cleaner than we have ever been before. However, no human being can ever promise us that we can be clean on the inside as well as the outside. Only our mighty God can do that!

He puts us through a cleansing and a purification that no scientist or inventor could ever produce. No matter how hard we scrub, only God has the ultimate catharsis. Jesus died on the cross and spilled His blood so that His pure and holy blood could erase our sin and bring about our eternal cleansing from sin. He alone can purge us inside and make us whiter than snow.

Long before Christ came to earth, Isaiah wrote this, "Come now, let's settle this, says the Lord. Though your sins are like scarlet, I will make them as white as snow. Though they are red like crimson, I will make them as white as wool" Isaiah 1:18 (NLT).

What do we have to do in order to receive this deep cleansing? "Believe on the Lord Jesus Christ and you will be saved" Acts 16:31 (NLT); And then John tells us once you believe that "if we confess our sins to Him, He is faithful and just to forgive us our sins, and to cleanse us from all wickedness" I John 1:9 (NLT). It is such a simple message, that many do not believe, because they want to be able to do something to earn their way into heaven. Nevertheless, God's way is to "only believe" and it really is that easy! His cleansing is one sure thing that you can receive free!

Personal Note:

We live in a time when we are always trying to get something for nothing. Nevertheless, every time we go down that path, we find that there is a price to pay. No lottery, or sweepstake or any other 'get-rich-quick' thing will ever really last. Even if we happen to win something, it never is enough. There is that feeling deep inside that something is still missing. There is always a catch.

With my heavenly Father, everything is different. He sent His Son as a free gift to cleanse me, purge me and purify my life All I had to do was believe and receive this gift of salvation. God has done so much for me. He has brought a rich, full and free life, which is the most satisfying life I could possibly live. He promises that my life in Him will be everything I have ever dreamed. John tells us, "I have come that they may have life, and that they may have it more abundantly" John 10:10b (NKJ). My being is overflowing with a guilt-free life that He has cleansed. How awesome!

Prayer:

Father, thank You so much for the free gift of Your Son, Jesus Christ. My heart is full of gratitude and love for welcoming me into Your heavenly family and cleansing me from sin! In His name, Amen.

Your Reflections:

Day 77

God is . . . The Guardian of Peace

Bible Reading: Philippians 4:1-8

As I am writing this, it is the Christmas season. All around me are constant reminders of all of the bounty that is available to give to someone on my Christmas list. Sometimes, this season is riddled with trying to find the perfect gift for each person. It can become very stressful and create problems among family and friends.

Our society has become so "gift" conscious that we tend to forget about the One who came to earth to give us the greatest gift of all. We can become so stressed that we forget that Christ came as the Prince of Peace. That is the essence of His message to us.

There are many ways that we can lose our peace. Even in our everyday living. We can forget all of the blessings and dwell on the fussy little irritations that interfere in our lives every day.

In Philippians, Paul is urging two women who had a disagreement, to settle their differences. They both had been a witness to help Paul pass on the good news of salvation. They both loved their Savior, but they had allowed discord to come between them. Paul gave them the solution to their problem. It is the same solution in our times of stress today, as well. He wrote, "Don't worry about anything; instead pray about everything. Tell God what you need, and thank Him for all He has done. Then you will experience God's peace, which exceeds anything we can understand. His peace will guard your hearts and minds as you live in Christ" Philippians 4:6, 7 (NLT).

Personal Note:

My mother used to tell me repeatedly, "I sure wish I could shut my mind off; it goes twenty-four hours a day." She lived well into her 80's; and she was a wonderful example to me of her faith in our Lord and Savior. Unfortunately, I seem to have the same problem she did. It seems that my mind goes 24-7. I cannot taste of God's complete peace until I learn to not only turn my heart over to Him, but my mind as well.

I have always been super active! I suppose that if they diagnosed things back when I grew up, I may have had ADHD. I never sat still. I had trouble focusing and still do, at times. This is one area that I have worked very hard to allow God to control.

It was not until I started having prolonged quiet times with my Father that I felt at ease and peaceful. He is the creator of peace, and He tells me that He is also the guardian of my heart and mind. I am learning to turn my mind over to Him and allow Him to guard it and bring me peace.

He does that so beautifully when I allow Him to control it. I have to admit that during this holiday season, I have not allowed His peace to penetrate my mind as much as I should, but I have a week left before Christmas, and I am inviting the Prince of Peace to enter my mind anew and bring me the peace that only He can bring. What a blessing He has for me when I allow His peace to guard my heart and mind!

Prayer:

Father, I know that You will keep me in perfect peace when I allow You to guard my heart and my intellect. Help me to let You enter my thoughts and my mind. How grateful I am that You are the guardian of my life. My Prince of Peace. In Your name, Amen.

Your Reflections:

Day 78

God is . . . Harmony

Bible Reading: 1 Peter 3:8-12

All nature sings of the harmony that God created in this glorious world. It is so evident in the majesty of the high mountain peaks to the verdant valleys as they come alive in magnificent color to bathe the earth in their glory. The ocean is filled with power and beauty as its wave's crash to the shore. Each blends in beautiful harmony of praise to its Creator.

Yes, God's synchronization is firmly established in all creation, except man. The one form of creation that should be in the tightest accord with each other is often in conflict. Everything God does is in perfect harmony, yet we cannot seem to live harmoniously on this earth. When Adam and Eve sinned, everything changed. We do not know how their marriage was, but we do know that their own children were at odds with each other; and Cain became the very first murderer. We have gone downhill from there.

Regrettably, Christians struggle with this as well. Even when the church was young, the Apostles taught about harmony or the lack thereof. Peter wrote, "Finally, all of you, live in harmony with one another; be sympathetic, love as brothers, be compassionate and humble" 1 Peter 3:8 (NLT). As believers, we are told, very directly, to live in agreement with one another. Yes, the world is a beautiful place when it works harmoniously together. That is exactly what we were created to do!

Personal Note:

I used to sing in "Sweet Adeline's," a women's barbershop organization. I was in a chorus and several quartets as well. You learn quickly to blend your personalities as well as your voices because to create a perfect harmony in acappella music, you not only feed off of each other's notes, but you feed off each other's attitudes.

My good friend, Dani and I sang together for many of those years. We learned to blend our personalities and voices early on. She and I are still ardent friends today. Because of the close bond that we have shared, we actually have become more like sisters. Unfortunately, that is not always the case in all quartets. I have seen some of our championship quartets miss that longed-for medal, simply because they had not learned to blend the personality with the voice.

God created each of us unique. When we are in His family, however, we need to be in perfect harmony, so that our personalities can bring music to His ears. Learning to live in one accord has brought blessing into my life, and that is what God intended.

Prayer:

Father, how beautifully You have created all nature as an example of the harmony that is available to me when I allow You to blend my personality with another. Help me to live in unity of spirit as I learn to meld with other Christian sisters and brothers. In Jesus' name, Amen.

Your Reflections:

Day 79

God is . . . Our Rest

Bible Reading: Hebrews 4:1-7

From my journal on September of 2002: "I am having a difficult time right now with peace and rest. As we are in the process of moving from our apartment into our home, there seem to be new developments or situations every day. Trying to move into what I hope will be our last home, trying to sell our condominium in Newport, Oregon; incorporating the combination of three homes and trying to keep Dad as comfortable and uninvolved as we can, while we juggle all of our challenges, is mind boggling. I have a difficult time trying to find rest for my soul."

I think we have all been in circumstances that, at times, seem to consume our attention and keep us from resting in God's peace. Paul had some things to say about rest. In Hebrews, he writes, "God's promise of entering His rest still stands, so we ought to tremble with fear that some of you might fail to experience it. For this good news—that God has prepared this rest—has been announced to us just as it was to them. But it did them no good because they didn't share the faith of those who listened to God" Hebrews 4:1-2 (NLT).

The rest that Paul talked about was the promise of God to the Israelites, when they entered the Promised Land that they would live in peace and rest as long as they obeyed God's laws, and did not turn away from them. God will give us this same peace when we turn our stresses completely over to Him and trust in His promise to us that He will give us rest.

Jesus talked about this rest when He said, "Come to me, all of you who are weary and carry heavy burdens and I will give you rest" Matthew 11:28 (NLT). We need only to believe His promise and turn our situation over to Him. He alone can bring us rest as we are going through chaos. It takes us back again to the obedience of trusting Him and abiding and remaining in Him.

Personal Note:

Why is it so hard to turn my stresses immediately over to Him? I think it is that I get into a rhythm of starting through the situation and I do not seek His face before I get involved in whatever is creating my stress.

We just went through the Christmas season and it seems like every year we have more sickness and demanding situations come upon us during this time of year, than at any other. It is the season when we set aside a special day to remember the birth of our Savior, the Prince of Peace, yet we seem to worship the prince of pressure instead.

Paul reminds us, "For all who have entered into God's rest have rested from their labors, just as God did after creating the world—so let us do our best to enter that rest. But if we disobey God as the people of Israel did, we will fail" Hebrews 4:10-11 (NLT). I need a constant reminder to rest in His care, to obediently turn over my busyness and burdens to Him so that He can give me rest. How I need His rest, today!

Prayer:

Father, You spoke so directly to me today. Forgive me for not seeking Your peace at this challenging time of year. Help me to trust You and turn over my burdens to You before they become stresses. I thank You that You came to bring peace, because You are the Prince of peace! In Your name, Amen.

Your Reflections:

Day 80

God is . . . A New Beginning

Bible Reading: James 4:7-10

What is the Christian life all about? As soon as we accept Christ as our Savior and ask Him to forgive us of all our sins, He does so and we become Christians. Does it end there? Do we have to live differently once we have made that decision, or do we just continue to live our lives the same as before?

From Acts to Revelation the Apostles begin to teach us what it means to live the Christian life. James confronts what it means to be a Christian, head on! "What good is it, dear brothers and sisters, if you say you have faith but don't show it by your actions? Can that kind of faith save anyone?" James 2:14 (NLT). He goes on to tell us how important it is to show we have faith, by our actions. We need to model our lives after Christ and learn to walk in His ways.

One of the greatest obstacles to our Christian faith is people who do not "practice what they preach." They talk a good story, but their lives do not reflect any change, or worse still, they actually act worse than those who do not claim to be Christians.

James reminds us that we need to be very careful not only of our actions but also of our speech. We need to be reminded that our actions speak more loudly than our words. We can be judgmental, angry and vicious if we do not watch our tongues.

Living the Christian life is not always easy, but we can start over with our Father anytime that we humble ourselves. When we are truly repentant, there is always forgiveness. James tells us in verse 10 (NLT), "Humble yourself before the Lord and He will lift you up in honor." God always responds to a humble heart. He will always be there to give us a new beginning. How grateful I am that He has lifted me up repeatedly as I learn to walk in His ways.

Personal Note:

As I search my own life, I know that there has been growth in this area. He is a God of new beginnings; and no matter what I have done or how often I have failed Him, when I come humbly before Him in true repentance, He will always forgive me and allow me to begin again. He rejoices in a repentant heart.

I do not have to return to the starting line, He just has me start anew and afresh with Him where I am right now. He lifts me up and places me right where I was before I got off the path and fills me with renewed strength in Him. Then I continue on the rocky upward slope to new blessing and healing. What a loving Father!

Prayer:

Father, thank You for being a God of complete forgiveness and fresh starts. You know my frailties and You forgive my shortcomings. I praise You for knowing everything about me and forgiving me when I come humbly before You. How I love You! In Jesus' name, Amen.

Your Reflections:

Day 81

God is . . . Right Living

Bible Reading: Titus 2:1-8

Sometimes when we have been Christians a long time, we get lazy and think we know everything there is to know about the Christian faith. It is common to see senior Christians just sitting back silently and letting the "younger folk" do the work of the church, or even becoming inactive in the work of our Father.

What is my role in God's kingdom, as I get older? Titus makes it very clear. As an older woman, I am directed to "be reverent in the way I live, not to be slanderers or addicted to much wine, but to teach what is good" Titus 2:3 (NIV).

That does not sound like I am to be put out to pasture and just sit and do nothing more spiritually. No! Titus goes on to say that, we should teach the younger women by our example how to live righteous lives in their homes as well as in church. We are to pass on the wisdom that we have learned through the years of service to our Lord and Savior.

If we live our lives in obedience to God's Word, our very actions can instruct our younger brothers and sisters in right living. Our purpose is to honor God. We do that by our obedience to Him. He has a real purpose for us, as we get older. Titus wrote, "For the grace of God has been revealed, bringing salvation to all people. And, we are instructed to turn from godless living and sinful pleasures. We should live in this evil world, with wisdom, righteousness, and devotion to God while we look forward with hope to that wonderful day when the glory of our great God and Savior, Jesus Christ will be revealed. He gave His life to free us from every kind of sin, to cleanse us, and to make us His very own people, totally committed to doing good deeds" Titus 2:11-15 (NLT). I am so grateful, as an older Christian, to be an example to my younger sisters but it is also a great responsibility that I do not take lightly!

Personal Note

How wonderful to know that I can still be very effective and important in God's kingdom. Too many senior citizens retire and then have no purpose or goals in their lives. They just sit around watching TV and do not pass on the gems of wisdom to the younger generation who could learn so much from their lives.

It brings me a great deal of hope and joy to know that I can serve my Savior until the day He takes me home to be with Him forever. I can be a role model to my younger Christian friends as well as those who have not yet come to know the Savior Who has changed my life so dramatically.

I am honored that He has given me this project along with other work to be done for Him. I know that as I obey Him, step by step along His way, that my life will really count for Him both now and for eternity! There is nothing greater than that!

Prayer:

Father, thank You for putting Your trust in me to pass on to others Your ways of right living. You are so awesome in Your dealings with me. Help me to be obedient to every call that You have made in my life. In my blessed Savior's name, Amen.

Your Reflections:

Day 82

God is . . . Restoration

Psalm 85:1-7

Restoration walks hand in hand with forgiveness. Whenever we go through a misunderstanding or have been deeply hurt by someone, we cannot feel peace with that person until we truly forgive them. If we have been wounded in spirit, it is hard to accomplish forgiveness and true restoration in that relationship. In fact, sometimes a family member or close friend will go through their entire life without forgiving the one who hurt them so deeply. They usually end up full of bitterness and resentment.

When our hearts are breaking, only a God, who instantly forgives us and sends our transgressions as far as the east is from the west to never remember them again, can bring us true restitution in a relationship. David knew about restoration. He cried out to God, "Now restore us again, O God of our salvation. Put aside your anger against us once more . . . Won't You revive us again, so Your people can rejoice in You? Show us Your unfailing love, O Lord, and grant us Your salvation" Psalm 85:4, 6, 7 (NLT).

God will hear our plea every time if we come before Him with a repentant heart. However, He also requires us to forgive those who have hurt us. If we cannot forgive others, He cannot forgive us. He will bless us abundantly when we truly forgive those who hurt us, when we can restore (at least to some degree) that relationship again. It is so important, especially if it is a spouse, family member, or good friend. We are not to build up resentment no matter how much we hurt each other. The sooner we can "clear the air" and re-establish our relationships, the sooner God can restore us and fill us with His unfailing love. I love what the Psalmist wrote as we continue reading this wonderful Psalm, "Unfailing love and truth have met together. Righteousness and peace have kissed! Truth springs up from the earth and righteousness smiles down from heaven" Psalm 85:10-12 (NLT). That is true restoration!

Personal Note:

I cannot tell you how many times I have needed to come before my Father and ask for His forgiveness. It has been a process, however, to be able to forgive others as easily. I have had to go through some tough times to learn to have a truly forgiving heart. I can tell you, though, as I have learned to forgive, it has brought me to the knowledge of how much I need God's restoration in my own life.

When I hear someone tell me something about another believer, it always makes me look into my own heart. Nevertheless, when I do, I know that I cannot judge that other person because I am a long way from perfection in my own life.

I am so grateful that God's unfailing love reaches down, forgives me every time, and restores my soul. Righteousness and peace can kiss, and truth can spring up in my heart!

Prayer:

Thank You, Father for Your forgiveness and restoration. Help me to forgive others and restore relationships in my life. Keep me from bitterness and resentment, so that Your righteousness and peace can revive my heart, as I trust You. In the mighty name of Jesus, Amen.

Your Reflections:

Day 83

God is . . . Offering His Sheltering Wings

Bible Reading: Psalm 91:1-7

If you have ever seen a mother hen protect her young, it is an amazing sight. The mother will slowly gather her chicks, one by one until she has them all safely harbored under her wings. Nothing can harm them when they are nice, cozy, and warm under her protective feathers. Jesus talked about this very thing when He looked down on His precious children, His beloved city of Jerusalem, "O Jerusalem, Jerusalem, you who kill the prophets and stone those sent to you, how often I have longed to gather your children together, as a hen gathers her chicks under her wings, but you were not willing" Luke 13:34 (NIV).

Our Father wishes to protect us, as well. I have this wonderful image of these massive feathery iridescent wings that reach out to encompass every one of His children. They are so beautiful and so enormous that there is always plenty of room left for one more child. He will gently beckon us to come under His protective wings.

The Psalmist wrote several times about these magnificent wings, "He will cover you with His feathers. He will shelter you with His wings. His faithful promises are your armor and protection" Psalm 91:4. (NIV). What a glorious picture of how very much He cherishes us.

Whenever we are going through a hard place in our lives, I am sure that our heavenly Father opens His glorious wings and says something like, "Come under my protection, my child. I know that you are going through some difficult things right now, but I am your refuge. I am your safety. Come, snuggle under my wings, I will be your shelter through the storm."

David wrote, "For if you make the Lord your refuge, if you make the Most High your shelter, no evil will conquer you, no plague will come near your home. For He will order His angels to protect you wherever you go" Psalm 91:9-11 (NLT). What a fabulous promise!

Personal Note:

I have been under those protective wings many times. When I call upon Him, He gathers me under His feathers; and even though the storm may be raging and my heart may be breaking, He protects me from being battered against a rock and destroyed.

When I relax and abide under His wings, I have peace in my heart as I safely go through the hard time. Oh how it must break His heart, though, when I forget to run to those magnificent wings and I try to handle the situation on my own. I am sure that He must be saying, "Child of mine, come! Run toward my soft billowy wings! I long to comfort you!"

Prayer:

Oh, my Father, help me to nestle safely under Your wings where I know You will protect and keep me. You alone bring peace to my troubled heart. How I thank You for Your shelter in times of turbulence. You are my help and safety! How I praise You for Your comfort. In Jesus' powerful name, Amen.

Your Reflections:

Day 84

God is . . . The Right Path

Bible Reading: Psalm 25: 4-10

It seems to me that as every year goes by, it becomes harder for many, to live a pure and holy life. Our culture is filled with everything that diverts us from living morally, and encourages us to do whatever we please. Anything goes! Teenagers face challenges today, which I never even knew existed when I was growing up. Our televisions and computers are packed with every kind of perversion.

We have seen a steady decline in morality and values in the last fifty years that is staggering. How confusing it must be for our children who are taught one thing at home, and another thing by their peers and educators. David wrote often, crying out to God to forgive him for wrong thinking and keep him on the right path, "Show me the right path, O Lord; point out the road for me to follow. Lead me by Your truth and teach me, for You are the God who saves me. All day long I put my hope in You" Psalm 25:4-5 (NLT).

How can we know the right path? By reading God's Word and learning from Him. He is our teacher. He loves us to ask Him to guide us. After all, He not only made us, He made everything good that exists. It is only logical that He would be the One we seek for direction in living our lives.

Many times our life becomes chaotic before we approach our Lord to help straighten it out. However, He is always merciful to us if we come to Him with a repentant heart. "The Lord is good and does what is right; He shows the proper path to those who go astray. He leads the humble in doing right, teaching them His way" Psalm 25:8, 9 (NLT). He alone is our "right path."

Personal Note:

We recently changed our television watching from a cable system to a satellite system. Although it has brought a lot of good programming to us, some of the commercials and content are displaying very perverted things. I now record most of the programs so I can fast forward through the commercials, but if my five year old grandson were here, even though the program he might watch could be innocent, I would have to be very careful and selective in allowing him to watch TV at all.

I remember in the fifties when we watched family programs, where it was not allowed to even suggest that a man and woman would sleep in the same bed. "I Love Lucy" is a good example; she and Ricky even had twin beds. We have wandered a long way down from that path! The more I keep my mind on godly things, the less likely I am going to be exposed to wrong thinking. David wrote, "My eyes are always on the Lord, for He rescues me from the traps of my enemies." Psalm 25:15 (KJV). I am very selective in what my eyes watch. My heart yearns to keep on the right path and allow God to teach me His ways.

Prayer:

Father, even though I am surrounded by evil all around, I know that when I come humbly before You, my Teacher, that You will show me the right path and right living. Thank You for directing my life. In Jesus' name, Amen.

Your Reflections:

Day 85

God is . . . My Lawyer

Bible Reading: Lamentations 3:55-60

I have not needed a lawyer very often in my life, and I am very grateful for that. In our society, it can be costly and frightening to stand before a judge, have a lawyer standing by your side that will plead your case, and then hope for a fair judgment in the end.

Jeremiah had been pleading the case for Judah for forty years. He would be in anguish over the sinfulness of God's people and beg them to repent, but nobody listened. His life was certainly not posh and pampered. He was rejected, thrown in prison, taken against his will to Egypt and then thrown in a cistern to die. Nevertheless, in everything he remained faithful as God's representative, and by God's standards, Jeremiah was a huge success.

After being faithful to God all those years, we read in Lamentations how Jeremiah was finally asking God to plead his case for him. "Lord, you are my lawyer! Plead my case! For You have redeemed my life. You have seen the wrong they have done to me Lord, be my judge and plead me right" Lamentations 3:58-59 (NLT).

Jeremiah did not mess around with shoddy lawyers. No! He went to the One and only One who could plead his case. After all, God knew everything about him. Jeremiah had lived such a life in front of His God, that he did not have any trouble asking God to be his lawyer. What an astounding request!

It gives me pause as I think of my own life. Because of Christ, I can come before my God and ask Him to be my lawyer—to plead my case and my Lord promises to do just that! John wrote, "My dear children I am writing this to you so that you will not sin. However, if anyone does sin, we have an advocate who pleads our case before the Father. He is Jesus Christ, the One who is truly righteous" I John 2:1 (NLT). How incredible! How divine!

Personal Note:

This is amazing to me because He promises that all I need to do is ask Him for anything that pleases Him, and He will hear and answer my request. "We are confident that He hears us when we ask for anything that pleases Him. And since we know He hears us when we make our requests, we also know that He will give us what we ask for" I John 5:14, 15 (NLT). It pleases Him for me to ask for His forgiveness of my sin.

The same applies when we have been harmed or wronged by others. When I have been hurt or misunderstood by someone, too many times I have just stood by, taken the abuse, and internalized it holding on to the pain. I must admit that most of my life I never thought about asking God to plead my case for me.

How comforting it is to know that when I have been wrongly accused, hurt by others or even mistreated, I can ask my heavenly Father to plead my case, make things right and He will do it every time. I may not see the outcome from a human point of view, I may never know until I get to heaven; but every move I make, every step I take, God is carefully keeping track, and He is the best lawyer I could ever have.

Prayer:

Father, thank You for consistently teaching me Your ways. Thank You, my Father, that You have the best lawyer available to me upon my request—Christ Jesus, my Redeemer and my Lord. In His powerful name, Amen.

Your Reflections:

Day 86

God is . . . A Lover of Solitude

Bible Reading: Matthew 14:13-15, 22-23

Solitude, what a wonderful thing it is when we have had a stressful day and finally have free time to refresh our body, mind and spirit. A part of our lives is easily ignored. God gave us guidance right from the beginning, when He took a day off from creation to rest. Jesus, when He was here on earth, gave us a good example of how hard it can be to find solitude. Yet He kept thinking ahead and found time to do it because it was an important part of living a healthy life.

Jesus' cousin, John, had just been beheaded; and when the disciples found out, they went to tell Jesus. As soon as Jesus heard the news, He withdrew into a solitary place. However, the multitude found out where He was, and one of His most famous miracles—the feeding of the five thousand was performed there.

Even though His heart was breaking and He needed rest, He had compassion on the people and insisted that His disciples feed them before they were sent away. It was getting close to nightfall; and Christ knew they were all hungry. Again, He sought solitude. "Jesus insisted that His disciples get back into the boat and cross to the other side of the lake, while He sent the people home. After sending them home, He went up into the hills by Himself to pray. Night fell while He was there alone" Matthew 14:22-23 (NLT).

He knew that He must find time while He had it, because another one of His miracles was about to transpire. His disciples were in trouble. A strong wind had arisen, and they were fighting heavy waves. How frightening it must have been for them out in the open sea, in the darkness of the night with a storm surrounding them.

"About three o'-clock in the morning Jesus came toward them walking on the water. They were terrified because they could not see Him clearly. He immediately calmed them and said, "Don't be afraid, take courage, I am here!" Matthew 14:25-27 (NLT). Jesus took care of quieting not only the disciples, but the angry sea as well, nevertheless He had taken time first to rest and talk to His Father in prayer, so that He was refreshed before He calmed the disciples and the sea.

Personal Note:

What a marvelous example this is to me. When life gets too stormy and rough for me to handle, I need to come to the place of solitude. My heavenly Father is waiting for me to come to Him. He alone can calm the angry sea of my life.

It is of utmost importance when life is bombarding me from all sides that I come to God in prayer. He has never failed to console me when I stop the rush and take time to come before Him for solace. He will always gently say, "Don't be afraid, take courage, I am here." Nothing can bring more peace and rest to my body, mind and spirit than that!

Prayer:

Father, thank You for Your compassion and comfort. In the solitude of Your unfailing love and strength, I can rest and receive refreshment for my soul. Thank You for the peace that only You can bring to my troubled heart. In Jesus' name I pray, Amen.

Your Reflections:

Day 87

God is . . . Leading North

Bible Reading: Deuteronomy 2:1-7

How cozy it is sometimes to be in my comfort zone. I get up, make a cup of coffee, go into my living room, have my prayer time and Bible reading, go back to the kitchen, eat my breakfast, go into my office, start writing and researching material and doing my various routines.

Sometimes my life becomes disrupted with too many phone calls, unexpected crises, and multiple interruptions. When that happens, I am OK for a while but if it goes on too long, I begin to feel stressed. If I turn immediately to my heavenly Father, He helps me manage things and life becomes comfortable again. Most of these pressures are simply life pressing upon me, but there are times when God changes my routine and my anxiety increases.

That is what happened to the children of Israel. They had disobeyed God and consequently had to wander in the wilderness for 40 years. Moses wrote, "Then we turned around and headed back across the wilderness toward the Red Sea, just as the Lord had instructed me, and we wandered around in the region of Mount Seir for a long time" Deuteronomy 2:1 (NLT). A trip that was meant to take only a few weeks endured for 40 years!

I imagine that the Israelites became very comfortable in the wilderness after such a long time. Just when they thought, the Promised Land may not be that great and seemed content, God spoke to Moses again. "Then at last the Lord said to me, you have been wandering around in this hill country long enough, turn to the north" Deuteronomy 2:2 (NLT). I imagine there was quite a stir in the camp that day. Going forth into the unknown is always daunting, but God always knows the right time to turn something good into something better, but it inevitably takes faith and obedience to Him before it can be realized.

I can be nestled in and not want to progress within my spiritual life. I just went through one of those phases and they are usually painful because I can become warm and cozy in my spiritual growth and do not always want to move on.

However, my heart's desire is always to move ever closer to my Lord because "our citizenship is in heaven, from which also we eagerly wait for the Savior, the Lord Jesus Christ" Philippians 3:20 (NAS). "So even if I don't want to, (and I am struggling right now), but God needs to move me to the north, I know that He will prepare me and help me to be ready to step out again and move in His direction."

Personal Note:

It is very easy for me to be content to live right where I am. Physically, my husband Don and I have moved so many times that I do not relish that experience again. Emotionally it is a very disruptive place to be and spiritually I am never eager to move out of my comfort zone. Moving is just not a natural thing that I enjoy doing! In fact, I read in a survey that moving is considered among the top five most stressful events in life.

No matter how much I dread it, spiritually, my Father has asked me yet again to leave my comfort zone and move forward in writing this book. There are days when I don't want to continue on this path. It can be very uncomfortable. Sometimes what God has led me to discuss is very painful because it hits close to home. No matter how much I yearn to do what God has called me to do, I prefer the grassy knoll of comfort rather than ascending the mountain to the north where I have never been before. No matter how hard it might be for me to go, I know I must precede northward where God can continue to direct my path!

Prayer:

Father, You are so amazing. All I need to do is trust You and allow You to guide me. Help me to continue to listen to You, so that I will hear Your direction when I am changing course and You want me to go north again. How I love You! In Jesus' name, Amen.

Your Reflections:

Day 88

God is . . . Fond of Joyful Living

Bible Reading: Philippians 1:3-9

Living in obedience to God is living in joy! In my life, I find that I cannot live in joy and be negative or depressed at the same time. My solution is that if I am feeling down about something, I need to search my heart and see where I have backed away from allowing God to be at the heart of my day. I am not talking about the difficulties that come into our lives that we do not have any control over. I am talking about my everyday routine where I have God as my center.

I may have started the day off with Him, and then suddenly I find that I am frustrated and feeling pressured. When I really examine my feelings, I usually find that my joy diminished because I tried to handle something in my own way, not God's way.

Paul is such a wonderful example of living the life of joy no matter what. He suffered terrible persecution and some of his most joy-filled writings happened while imprisoned for preaching the gospel. He writes, "So it is right that I should feel as I do about all of you for you have a special place in my heart. You share with me the special favor of God, both in my imprisonment and in defending and confirming the truth of the Good News" Philippians 1:7 (NLT).

I can feel the joy in Paul's life. He did not sit around moaning about how bad he had things. On the contrary, suffering for his Savior, was absolute joy. You sense that joy in most of His writings. "And I want you to know, my dear brothers and sisters that everything that has happened to me here has helped to spread the Good News" Philippians 1:12 (NLT). Everything about Paul's life was positive and full of joy.

When I am around someone who is truly living for God, he or she is a true joy. They are secure, positive thinkers, peaceful and content; and it usually rubs off on me. It is hard to be down in your spirit when you are around a truly joyful Christian. They are like a magnet. We gravitate toward them and want what they have. "If you have any encouragement from being united with Christ, if any comfort from His love, if any fellowship with the Spirit, if any tenderness and compassion, then make my joy complete by being like-minded, having the same love, being one in spirit and purpose" Philippians 2: 1-2 (NIV).

Personal Note:

I want my life to be an encouragement and become a magnet that draws others to me because I live the life of God's joy and blessing. Some of us are just naturally joyful, while others must work a little harder to have God's joy shining through our lives. For me, this is a real goal. To have my countenance shine forth His beauty; and be full of joyful living, abiding in Him, so that I might be a blessing to all those I am around. It is a goal worth achieving!

Prayer:

Father, make my life bring forth Your joy that I may show Your true nature to all who are around me. Forgive me for grumbling and complaining. Fill my life with joyful living. In Christ's name, Amen.

Your Reflections:

Day 89

God is . . . Our Ultimate Health Plan

Bible Reading: Deuteronomy 30:15-20

I have always had the deepest respect and a thankful heart when I am healthy and feeling well. I have never had a strong immune system and have had chronic bronchitis my entire life. I have been hospitalized more times than I can count and had several surgeries as well as a blood disorder. Through it all however, I consider myself healthy. God has been very gracious to me as I am learning His ways.

He told us in Deuteronomy what it would take to have His blessing on our lives. "Now listen! Today I have given you the choice between life and death, between blessings and curse. Now I call on heaven and earth to witness the choice you make. Oh, that you would choose life, so that you and your descendants might live! You can make the choice by loving the Lord your God, obeying Him, and committing yourself firmly to Him. That's the key to your life!" Deuteronomy 30:19-20a (NLT).

As I am growing in Him, I am learning to eat healthier foods. No matter what diet is out there, most nutritionists provide us a similar formula. Eat whole grains, fruits and vegetables; drink plenty of water, and exercise! They differ in the details but this is a common thread. In all of the diets that I have been on, it has only been in the past two or three years that I had a strong desire to eat as God directed me through Scripture. Several books on health are biblically based and that is what I want to use in my future eating plan.

As I become more knowledgeable about God's health plan, I realize that I have not paid attention to taking care of my physical body the way that I should. He laid down a plan for the Israelites to follow to remain healthy and He has that same formula for me today. Deuteronomy 30:20 reads, "If you love and obey the Lord, you will live long in the land the Lord swore to give your ancestors, Abraham, Isaac and Jacob" (NLT). I know that as I yield more to His will and obtain knowledge, he will bless me and give me a long life to serve Him.

Personal Note:

Much of my life I did not have a true understanding of health issues. Like many of us, I lived a life of fast food and not much in activity. I have paid a heavy price for that. I now realize that it is not about how I look, it is about how I take care of His temple. The laws that Moses set down by the hand of God, give me a great deal of instruction about diet, exercise and living a clean and pure life.

There is another verse in Deuteronomy that has really "hit home" for me. "The Lord our God has secrets known to no one. We are not accountable for them, but we and our children are accountable forever for all that He has revealed to us, so that we may obey all the terms of these instructions" Deuteronomy 29:29 (NLT). Powerful words! By His mercy, and my awareness, I will become better acquainted with His ways on health.

We now live in a retirement village where meals are provided for us. The food is well prepared but not always a balanced plan. This is a new challenge as I learn to adjust into a healthier life of diet and exercise. I am so grateful that God has provided this wonderful opportunity.

Prayer:

Father, You know my struggle in this area. Help me to desire healthier foods and apply to my life, healthier habits. Teach me Your ways that I may be pure in body, soul and spirit. In Jesus' name, Amen.

Your Reflections:

Day 90

God is . . . An Approval Encourager

Bible Reading: John 5:36-44

It was not until very recently that I realized that during my entire life, I have felt rejection. As far back as I can remember, I was told by my mother that I had been an unwanted child. She always ended by saying, "But I am so glad we had you, because you have brought me so much joy."

My father was a police officer and had turned his back on the Lord long before I was born. He would often drink himself into a stupor, pass out on the couch and then go to work the next day. It was in this setting that God chose me to be born. While my mother was pregnant with me, my father who had again been drinking, took her up to a cliff at gunpoint, and wanted her to jump off to abort me. My mother refused; and since abortion was not an option, I am here today. I often wonder if that would be the case had laws been set in place to legalize abortion back then.

No matter how much or how little approval we get from those around us, our heavenly Father will always approve and reaffirm us. Jesus was the most rejected of all, yet He knew whose approval counted. His Father approved and that was all that was necessary. No one brought Christ more rejection and disapproval than the Jewish leaders. Jesus said, "Your approval means nothing to me because I know that you do not have God's love within you" John 5:41, 42 (NLT).

Approval seems more difficult for us. We live in a time when peer pressure and human approval seem to be all that matters. As our moral issues disintegrate, we seem increasingly insecure, and seek validation from others. Jesus said, "No wonder you can't believe! For you gladly honor each other, but you don't care about the honor that comes from the One who alone is God" John 5:44 (NLT). Yes, God's approval is positively what I want to focus upon.

Personal Note:

After I was born, my father was always kind and gentle with me. My sisters were about to start their teen-age years and I brought some comfort to both of my parents. God's timing is always perfect; and I believe that one of the reasons that I was born was to be an encouragement to both parents who would be facing a divorce by the time I was eight years old.

I told you this part of my story, because I believe there are so many hurting hearts facing rejection in their lives. When I finally realized that rejection was at the core of many of my struggles, it was as if God had poured out His healing balm on my heart and soul. I felt a sense of freedom that I had never experienced before.

I know this is a process in my life, in the same way that He is working out many other things within me. I now have a weapon against the wiles of Satan's lies. It is the truth of knowing that God's acceptance is far stronger than any false rejection that the enemy can throw at me. How I praise my loving heavenly Father who has opened the eyes of my heart and brought healing to my soul.

Prayer:

How precious You are to me, Father. You created me and planned every day of my life. Thank You for bringing me into the exact purpose that You have for me. I may need to go through some tough situations, but I know that my life is completely in Your control. I trust You, Father! In Jesus' name, Amen.

Your Reflections:

Day 91

God is . . . My Vinedresser

Bible Reading: John 15:1-7

I was born in the San Francisco Bay area in California. We had relatives that lived in Napa Valley, which is well known as wine country. I used to love to drive through that area and look at the immaculate vines as they were repeatedly pruned and tied, until they were submissive to what the vinedresser knew would be the best crop of grapes.

The vine is what growing grapes is all about—it is where the strength flourishes. The vine feeds the submissive branches until they are full and vital with real life flowing through them. Jesus referred to Himself as the true vine and His Father was the vinedresser. God breathes life into the vine, His Son Jesus Christ. Christ takes a stubborn willful branch, which will grow any direction left on its own, molds it, and coaxes it until He has the perfect yielding vine that will bear abundant fruit. "Yes, I am the vine; you are the branches. Those who remain in Me, and I in them, will produce much fruit" John 15:5 (NLT). Remaining, abiding, yielding, letting Christ work His work on this out-of-control branch is what will produce fruit.

In a vineyard, occasionally, no matter how careful a vinedresser may be, he finds a branch that will not respond to the pruning. The vinedresser will then cut it off destroying the branch. It is useless to the vineyard because it will not bear fruit. However, being supple in the hands of my heavenly Vinedresser, oh, the joy! I want to be pliable so that I can produce much fruit. John wrote, "When you produce much fruit, you are My true disciples. This brings great glory to the Father" John15:8 (NLT).

Personal Note:

Allowing God to completely fill me and bring a fullness of life to me is where I want to be. Residing in Christ takes trusting Him completely. It means that I have to relinquish my stubborn will and become flexible in His hands, so that He can shape me into the perfect fruit that I will one day become. I used to have the mistaken idea that bearing fruit was only winning souls to Christ, or doing great and mighty things for Him. I felt that my life did not measure up to the great and mighty. While showing others the way of salvation is the ultimate goal, our everyday lives count as well.

I have a purpose right here in my own little corner of the world. Everything that I do, every time I "stay in" the vibrancy and strength of the Vine, I am capable of bearing fruit. Things like remaining faithful every day in my schedule, raising my family, being a good wife and mother, or doing my job well and being honest in all my dealings, are all vital in His vineyard. Making godly choices and living in the uniqueness that God gave to only me, are all bearing fruit for Him if I am doing it for His glory and not mine.

Little things count for His kingdom as well. When I pass on a smile to someone who is sad, comfort a hurting heart, or encourage someone who is down in spirit, I bear fruit. Praying for another's needs, helping a little child, giving to the needy. are all little things that I can do daily to bear fruit. Producing fruit is simply doing God's will in my life. No branch is greater than another is. Faithfulness and obedience is what fills the branch with the vitality from the Vine. That is what helps show the lost souls the Way! That is my goal!

Prayer:

Father, thank You so much for being my Vinedresser. Continue to prune me and make me supple and yielding to Your blessed Son who is my Vine. Help me to bear much fruit for Your kingdom. In Christ's name, Amen.

Your Reflections:

****

claricefwlr@gmail.com